"For such a time
along in perfect ki
to realize that unless
there can be no Esthers for tomorrow. A good read for *princesses* in the making and their mothers.

—Linda Rios Brook
President, Lakeland Leadership League
Author, *Wake Me When It's Over, Lucifer's Flood,* and *Frontline Christians in a Bottom Line World*

Every girl is born with a deep longing in her heart to be desired. *Making of a Princess* expresses our Bridegroom God's burning passion to answer the deepest longings in our heart by revealing His affection for us. We are living in a generation with the greatest emotional brokenness in history. It is a critical hour for us to receive the revelation of God's fiery desire for us. Robin Rinke describes the journey of our heart of how God takes us in our weakness and makes us ready to be a suitable companion for the Bridegroom King. This book exposes the hindrances to our intimacy with Jesus and how we can overcome them. God has a plan for each one of us to come out of place of shame and into a place of dignity and royalty. Do you know who you are? Do you know what time of history you are living in? I beckon you to go on your journey and discover your destiny as a *princess* made ready for the King.

—Debra Hebert
IHOP Forerunner School of Ministry
International House of Prayer
Kansas City, Missouri

There is a tremendous need for a biblical basis to enhance a young woman's self esteem. Young women need to hear a different message than the one from television, peers, and books. Everything tells them something to the contrary to what Robin is trying to say. The world has a very different perspective on most important character qualities such as purity, self-control, and faithfulness. I recommend *Making of a Princess* to groups working with young women.

—DAWN SIEMON
WIFE OF JEFF SIEMON, NFL PLAYER
MINNESOTA VIKINGS
MOTHER OF THREE DAUGHTERS

The Making of a Princess is excellent in that it ties Robin's personal story with the Bible and the whole journey women must make from little girls to *princesses.* The reflections aspects are good for drawing things out. This book is long overdue.

—JOHN BAUDHUIN
FAMILY COUNSELOR
ASSISTANT PASTOR AND SENIOR COUNSELOR
COVENANT CENTRE INTERNATIONAL
PALM BEACH GARDENS, FLORIDA

What an *awesome* book! I found *The Making of a Princess* exciting, funny, and very real. I laughed and I cried as I went with Robin on the *princess* journeys of her own life, while being able to relate it to my own. This book is definitely a must read for all girls, young and older alike. Hands down, this was the most fun and applicable book that I have ever read on how to walk free from bondage, receive healing, obtain power, and hold your head high in this life as a *princess* in the kingdom of God.

—ANGELA KLINE
GEORGIA STATE ADVISOR
INTERNATIONAL ASSOCIATION OF HEALING ROOMS
DIRECTOR, HEALING ROOMS OF GREATER ATLANTA

Making of a Princess is a positive, inspirational and "feel good" book, which effectively drives the point home that every girl is a *princess.* The questions at the end of the chapters are insightful and useful. I would have loved to read a book like this in my early teens.

—Maggie Moore
College Student, Princeton University

I went through a tough time in junior high. This book really hit me and I'm an adult. I could relate! I loved Robin's use of the biblical *princesses.*

—Nancy Withers
Christ Presbyterian Church, Edina, Minnesota
Mother of three teen daughters

The Making of a Princess

Robin R. Rinke

A Strang Company

THE MAKING OF A PRINCESS by Robin R. Rinke
Published by Creation House Press
A Strang Company
600 Rinehart Road
Lake Mary, Florida 32746
www.creationhouse.com

Cover design by Terry Clifton

Library of Congress Control Number: 2004109822
International Standard Book Number: 1-59185-641-8

04 05 06 07 08 — 987654321
Printed in the United States of America

I lovingly dedicate this book to five special princesses:

Grama Bea, the Queen of *Princesses.* Every part of your life was wrapped in love; it was deeper than the deep blue sea…I miss our chats, your laughter, and soft skin. Knowing you are with the King of kings makes me smile. Thank you for teaching me the importance of listening to others and walking in unconditional love.

Sophia, my firstborn *Princess.* The Father designed you beautifully inside and out. Wisdom and grace exude out of you like that of Queen Esther. When you sing the heavens open. When you dance He is your audience of one. He sees your passion for Him, and you ravish His heart. You are His beloved *Princess* and my precious jewel.

Phoebe, My second-born *Princess.* Your beauty and loyalty exceed them all. When you smile His brightness radiates the atmosphere and penetrates hearts. You are His prophetic voice of delight, truth, and purity for this generation. He placed in you the ability to speak with humor and clarity. He thoroughly enjoys being with you and rejoices over you with singing. His eye is ever on you, my darling little *Princess.*

Lori, my one and only little *Princess* Sister. In you He has obviously placed His heart of compassion. You know just what to do and how to do it with such excellence and ease. Thank you for teaching me how to enjoy being a girl and helping me see myself as a *Princess.* I remember when you were born and bringing you home from the hospital. My little five-year-old arms carefully held you in the front seat of the blue Chevy. I knew then you were a special package from God sent to this earth. And one more thing, nobody on this planet can make me laugh like you do.

Mom, my first *Princess* Mentor. You have not hidden or buried the unique abilities and talents that have been given to you by the Father. All my life I have watched you use them to bless others. At an early age I watched you fearlessly lead new ministries. Your example has taught me to do the same. Your understanding of hospitality is a precious gift. You serve like royalty and sparkle like a *Princess* should. I rise up and call you blessed!

Acknowledgments

To Chuck, my husband, best friend, and hero. You are an amazing man of God. Thank you for loving and supporting me these past twenty-five years. Your friendship, prayer, and love exemplify Jesus, my bridegroom King.

To Samuel, our outrageously talented and adorable son. You are my delight. Just thinking about how special you are warms my heart. You're my guy. Thanks for your encouragement during this process.

To Dad, my handsome earthly father. Thank you for your support in every area of life and especially with this book. Your love for me has made it easy to understand how much the Father loves me.

To Barb Shultz, for your red pencil work and editing out all my stupid grammar. I appreciate all that you have done for me. When I think of gentleness and kindness I think of you. What a true woman of God.

To David Sluka, for countless hours of editing and writing in the early stages of this project. You really pushed me to dig for excellence. I owe you three signed books for those adorable *Princesses* of yours.

To Audra Shafer-Shanaman, for helping me develop the question portion of the book. You really know your stuff...what an anointed teacher.

To Linda Brook, for your support, wisdom, and love.

Also thank you to Julie Ramsland, Youth Director, Colonial Church, Edina, Minnesota, for her invaluable insights, Leonard Flachman at Kirkhouse for His encouragement, Craig and Bev Roberts, Justin and Allison Feldman, Karen Wong, Dana and Randy Hanson...all my family and friends.

CONTENTS

Introduction: Once Upon a Time.com 1

1 Walking My Dock 13

2 The First Royal Family 21

3 Cinderella: the Fictional *Princess* 36

4 What Does a *Princess* Look Like Anyway? 59

5 Tamar: the Tainted *Princess* 78

6 You Were Born for Such a Time As This 96

7 Rest in Your Royalty 110

8 *Princess* Key #1: Guarding Your Heart 128

9 *Princess* Key #2: Repentance 145

10 *Princess* Key #3: the Holy Spirit 154

11 It Is Time for You to Walk the Dock 164

12 Going Into Your World 170

> The royal daughter [*Princess*] is all glorious within the palace; her clothing is woven with gold. She shall be brought to the King in robes of many colors; the virgins, her companions who follow her, shall be brought to You. With gladness and rejoicing they shall be brought; they shall enter the King's palace.
>
> —Psalm 45:13–15, Author's Paraphrase

It is *time* that we see ourselves in this light…as daughters all glorious in HIS eyes!

Introduction

ONCE UPON A TIME.COM

SHE WAS THE kind of girl that seemed to glide right into the "cool group" at school. You know the type: cheerleader, athletic. In eighth grade she won the all-around gymnastic title by her spunky backhand springs and tricky aerials. Her chestnut brown hair gleamed in the sun with the smell of Herbal Essence Shampoo. She had a smile that could win a crowd, complimented by her button nose with the perfect tilt. Her contagious laugh made others want to giggle along with her. She always made the B Honor Roll without studying.

The only reason she was eager to get up in the morning and go to school was to see her best friends and the boys. Yes, she was boy crazy. People were constantly telling her how fun she was to be around. She loved the positive attention.

Those cool group girls were like *princesses.* Their skinny bodies showed off the latest fashions, and their clear skin gleamed with perfectly applied make-up. In the lunch room, as they sat at the cool lunch table, I often wondered if I could become a part of their group if I acted and dressed like them. Somehow I believed this would solve all my problems. Sound familiar?

As I studied this girl, she and the cool group seemed to be almost fearless about experimenting with alcohol, drugs, and boys. From our point of view, teachers and parents had no idea about anything that was going on at school, dances, parties, and at Friday night games. I do not know—maybe they did know, and just pretended they did not know. There was a lot of rule breaking going on, with nobody getting caught. Sound familiar?

For two years not much changed. Her life seemed to just glide along in CoolGroupLand. She had a best friend and they were inseparable. Actually their relationship looked like a lot of fun. They worked at being popular, and retained their cool group status at the cool lunch table. Sound familiar?

However, I began noticing a change in her the year before we all began high school. She started to hang around with girls from the "burn out" group; she sneaked cigarettes in the bathrooms. We had labels for our social groups. Sound familiar?

Usually two such opposite social groups do not mix. I could not figure out what she was doing. Why the big change? Nothing else seemed different. I was always curious as to what caused her to go in that direction. Why was she willing to sabotage her cool group status? Maybe the cool group was not all it looked to be. I was too afraid to directly ask her these questions because of the possibility it would make me look stupid, and would jeopardize my own standing in the group. I left my questions unanswered. Shortly thereafter she changed schools. We lost contact.

Thirty years later, while I was surfing the 'net on my computer, an advertisement for chatting with old school friends popped up on my screen. I grabbed the chance to talk with CoolGirlGroup by "Instant Messaging" (IM), her IM was RRR1963. I was able to ask her these unanswered questions from my past. Her answers were unexpected.

By the way, instant messaging has been around forever. Even though the generation before you did not have cell phones or computers to communicate messages with, they still had good old fashion note passing. I remember using codes like B/F/A (Best Friends Always), F/F (Friends Forever), TTYL (Talk To You Later), SWAK (Sealed With A Kiss), ILUVU (I Love You), TGIF (Thank Goodness It's Friday), CYA (See Ya), P/W/B (Please Write Back), and so on...anyway, here is our IM conversation from that day:

Me: hey-howz it going?

RRR1963: good—real good

Me: mind if i ask U some questions about jr. high days?

RRR1963: no, go ahead....

Me: well- i always watched U from a distance in school—thinking it would B awesome 2 B Ur friend...

RRR1963: really-LOL!

Me: yeah-U seemed 2 hit jr. high like a pro—gliding right in 2 the cool group—how does that happen? did U have a plan?

RRR1963: funny—i am not sure how it happened either! i had no plan—just knew what 2 do and knew what i liked, and what i wanted—i had just come from a private elementary school and was a big fish in a little pond—i was popular and basically friends with the whole class—then jr. high came along—it was a public school, and i was a little fish in a big pond—i had 2 learn some new tricks 2 stay afloat—especially if i wanted 2 stay popular—and i definitely wanted popularity...

Me: hmmmmm interesting...your main goal was 2 remain popular?

RRR1963: yeah—2 B noticed—liked—popular—and 2 hang around other fun and exciting girls was important 2 me...

Me: what made U so confident that U belonged 2 the cool group?

RRR1963: i think being raised in a loving home built up my confidence and self-esteem 2 the point that it never crossed my mind that i couldn't B part of the so called 'cool group'...or anything else i wanted 2 B a part of...

Me: so-self confidence and high self-esteem made U feel like U could B-long wherever U wanted 2 B-long?

RRR1963: yeah—i guess that's it—however, that group of friends was a security blanket 4 me...4 me 2 lose them would have been a huge loss—like i said, being popular was important 2 me...i made it a priority—a very high priority—more important than anything.

Me: U always looked confident and happy...

RRR1963: looks can B deceiving...as long as my personality and looks kept me in the cool group i felt confident and happy—@ times i worried that my personality and looks weren't going 2 B enough and then i would not B popular—like the time when a really cute girl transferred 2 our school...it was during eighth grade...she obviously fit in2 our cool group. i remember feeling intimidated that she would take my place in the group. i had 2 B nice 2 her, but all the time worrying she would B more popular than me. it sounds sick now...but it is the truth...i started searching for something 2 give me validation and cool group permanence. My search lead me 2 experiment with smoking, alcohol, and drugs...i thought i needed something 2 keep me as an exciting friend...

Me: really—i would have never guessed any of this was going on...

Her: yeah—just looking @ people doesn't always give U the full picture—when i think of it now 4 me 2 have been on the outside of that group would have been hard on me—so i wanted 2 do anything 2 keep my place...

Me: what was so bad about being on the outside of the cool group?

RRR1963: at the time i thought being on the outside

of that group would make me a loser in other peoples eyes...we were mean 2 those not in our group, and i knew i did not want 2 take the chance i'd B on the other side getting teased...i do not think any of us wanted 2 B mean, but it was something we just did—we were self-absorbed. usually we would get laughs @ others expense—it is sad, but i think this is typical jr. high social life—who U were seemed 2 depend on who U hung around with—not much has changed...it was definitely "follow the leader" kind of stuff—everyone picks their leader.

Me: yeah—there R still different social classes and always will B—and it will always hold true that who we hang around is who we become most like...who we follow and allow 2 B our leader is an important decision.

RRR1963: yeah...U can say that again...

Me: then if it was so important 2 U 2 have that status Y did U sabotage Ur cool group spot by hanging around a totally different social group that last year of Jr. High?

RRR1963: WOW...interesting question. U were watching me!

Me: yeah...that is a question i have always wanted 2 ask U!

RRR1963: that year—right before we entered high school was tough 4 me...

Me: how?

RRR1963: some upset @ home was going on with my older brothers that were having a hard time finding their place in this world—lots of turmoil and hurt—my parents were busy trying 2 fix their problems—they were doing the best they knew how...it was a stressful time...

Me: what did that have 2 do with U?

RRR1963: any adverse situation that arises in a home affects the whole family---depending on how things are handled it can have good and bad outcomes...my brothers were hanging out with the "burn-outs" (the party crowd) over in the high school and i guess i was just following their lead—its common for younger siblings 2 copy their older—i think i fell through the cracks and was missing the attention i was used 2 getting @ home—i seemed 2 B creating bad attention 4 myself just 2 get attention from my parents and others.

Me: it must have been weird having 1 foot in the cool group and 1 foot in the burn-out group…

RRR1963: yeah—it was—i did not know where i belonged anymore—the burn-outs did not care who U were—they accepted anyone—which is a good thing, but @ the same time it was a "free 4 all"—do what U want—party when U want—that kind of mentality is dangerous. i felt like it made me look mature if i hung around them! LoL! at the same time my cool group seemed 2 B breaking up slowly and getting ready 4 the next big re-grouping of social groups called senior high…

Me: U sounded confused…and no one 2 talk 2, eh?

RRR1963: U got it—that was a true picture of the confusion inside of me @ that point—straddling the fence of 2 totally different social groups—emotionally i was not dealing with the upset @ home—and physically i still looked like a boy! some changes were taking place physically, but not like my friends! i was embarrassed 2 not B developing like the other girls—2 make matters worse, i was actually 1 year younger than my classmates—i went in2 first grade @ the age of 5—so i probably was right on schedule with the class i should have been in 4 my age—and being a petite person anyways really did not help! i also had some issues from childhood that needed 2 B dealt with and i did not know how 2 do that…i did not even know i needed 2 deal with it…i was in a crisis @ a crossroads and confused!

Me: Wow. U had a lot going on in ur little world! nobody knows what others R really going through unless they have been told—i would have never guessed...

RRR1963: true...actually this was the 1st time i wasn't sure if my personality could hold my place of popularity—even my personality was changing—everybody's was—my confidence in who i was seemed 2 B actually diminishing! it proves that high self esteem and confidence alone cannot hold U when the winds of adversity blow...i needed more...

Me: so what ever came of U? i remember U went 2 another high school...did U make it through the friendship crisis and home turbulence? do U still look like a boy? LOL! do U like how U turned out?

RRR1963: it all worked out—i made it through the wilderness of those trial years—i did go 2 another high school, which ended up being a good thing...and yes, everything grew in the physical department!...LoL!...i finally looked like a girl! but not until i was 14...seemed like 4 ever! LoL! The age 14 was a big year 4 me...that was the year i became a *princess*—which changed my life.

Me: glad it all worked out...a *princess*? Wow...what happened?

Whoa! Before we find out what happened, we need to examine the life of a *princess.*

Why is it that every girl dreams about being a *princess*? What is it about being a *princess* that is so attractive? In reality there are many categories of *princesses.* The first category would be the actual blue blood *princess* born into a royal family. She would have servants, limousines, glittery gowns, tea parties, exotic trips, French cuisine, jewels, gilded palaces, and of course, she always marries the charming prince. Who would not love that?

Another category would be the man-made *princesses* that Hollywood creates with perfectly shaped bodies adorned with furs and gowns. Or the runway fashion models you read about that wear designer clothing in

Paris, Milan, and New York. Their glamorous lifestyle can be followed in magazines and on television shows.

This last category is more about attitude than anything else. For lack of a better description, I will call them, "The social cool group *princesses*." They are probably the easiest category for us common people to relate to. Every school has them. They actually lead quite ordinary lives as far as *princesses* go, but are viewed to have more advantages than those outside their group. They generally have influence in their school, youth group, or whatever else they belong to. Thus, we have the three categories of *princesses*:

1. Royal *Princess*
2. Man-Made *Princess*
3. Social Cool Group *Princess*

Now, keep these three *Princess* categories in mind, and read the following questions:

1. If the lives of *Princesses* are so full of indulgences and glamour, why are so many of them unhappy?

2. What has happened to their self-esteem?

3. Why are so many blue-blood *Princesses* and their man-made counterparts anorexic, hating their natural bodies?

4. Why do so many runway models turn to drugs?

5. Why have they not remained married to their prince charming when it is supposed to be happily thereafter?

6. Why do cool group *Princesses* in school experiment with alcohol and drugs?

7. What is it in their past that is haunting them to not be content with their seemingly perfect lives?

Obviously, it is not just the title of *Princess* or its lifestyle that makes one eternally happy. We all still want to be *Princesses*, but only if we can truly live in the fullness of joy. While the majority of us may not have the worldly *Princess* lifestyle, with perfect bodies, blemish-free skin, family wealth, or designer labels hanging in our closets, is it possible to still have the title of *Princess*?

How is this possible? Who is this *Princess*? How can the blue-blood, man-made, CoolGroup girl, or any girl, wear the title *Princess* with assurance and permanence?

A Daughter of the Most High King

God, the heavenly Father and King of the universe, offers this title of *Princess* to women everywhere. Whether young or old, blue blood, man-made, cool group, or anyone else, you can be a *Princess*. The Father does not play favorites. This transformation supernaturally takes place when you become an heir of the royal Kingdom of God. As a Christian, the crowned title of *Princess* is yours to wear. This is a title that must be worn in your heart. Your very life will be transformed by wearing it. It is not a worldly title, but eternal, and is given to us through God's love. We simply have to accept this gift, which comes with many privileges and responsibilities.

Developing a royal daughter takes time. Learning your role is a process. I watched a movie with my daughters that had this very theme. It was about an ordinary girl who found her long lost father. He just happened to hold a royal position in England. Because of his title, she had to learn her position as a royal daughter. This did not happen overnight. Watching an ordinary New York girl learn the ropes of royalty was hilarious.

If you are His *Princess*, you too are a work in progress. Day by day the character of your Heavenly Father is being developed in you. You are being groomed for the day that He sends His Son Jesus to gather us as His bride... He is the Prince of Peace and we are the *Princess* bride. This day is soon approaching and we need to be ready.

How does a *Princess* in waiting get ready? Especially when she has never waited for a Prince before? Maybe you have heard foundational teachings about how to live a Christian life in regards to intimate prayer, passionate worship, and meditating on the Word of God. However, I would also like to suggest that listening to and learning from older godly women can be a huge key in your success as a *Princess*. Why? Because we have been there, done that, and have the papers to prove it! That is where I come in.... The Bible encourages younger women to listen and learn from the older godly ones. Through my own experiences I hope to help you avoid pitfalls in this *Princess* journey.

Whether you are pre-teen or 105, it is possible to walk as a *Princess* even when you do not feel like one. You can glide through all the seasons in your life, and enjoy the wild ride on that roller coaster with confidence...really! Or, you can stumble through the roller coaster line, get on, and close your eyes in fear, scream, panic, and eventually barf! I watched a girl do that once. Her life was anything but a *Princess* success story.

It really is my mission to help you go through life gracefully, regardless of your circumstances or age. I can show you how an intimate relationship with the Father,

Son, and Holy Spirit will change every area of your life for the good. The kingdom of God and His ways will enhance everything you do and give you valuable lessons you can use the rest of your *Princess* life.

Since His ways are always opposite to the natural world that we live in, studying the Bible helps us to understand His supernatural ways. As I take you into the lives of various *Princesses* in the Bible, His supernatural kingdom will become clearer and clearer to you. Learning His ways will always bring victory instead of defeat, love instead of hatred, and true peace and joy in your life. In today's world, these traits are priceless.

This book was designed to work as a group Bible study or as a personal devotional. At the end of each chapter you will find questions that will cause you to reflect personally on what you have just read. As you read the book on your own, take time to meditate on the questions and answer them. Be as honest as you possibly can with your answers. This will give you the optimum impact and growth this book offers.

If used as a group Bible study, set up a committed weekly meeting time for your group. Whether just two or thirty are in your group, it is important to stay committed to one another. The commitment of each group member will draw you close to each other and help accomplish the goal of this book. Reading the book without a group situation is just as valuable. You will gain kingdom wisdom either way.

Maybe you are thinking, "But I have never heard of this royal family of God thing, and I certainly do not see myself as a *Princess*." That is okay, just go ahead and read. What you are about to read will impact the way you see things, for the rest of your life.

Everybody wants to be a *Princess*. If you have no other *Princess* sisters to share this Bible study with, go forward anyway, and do the questions on your own. There is a reason and purpose you have this book in your hands.

You are about to understand the amazing privileges and favor of being part of God Almighty's royal family. Chapter by chapter this royal mystery will unfold. The eyes of your understanding will be opened to see what being in the Kingdom of God is all about. As this revelation of the kingdom of God takes root in your life, you will begin to walk in ways you have never walked before. Get ready to walk the runway—walking as a *Princess*...

Chapter 1

WALKING MY DOCK

I WAS A *PRINCESS* walking down the long dock at my home. Like most lake homes in Minnesota, our family had a dock on the beach that extended into the water. Spring, summer, and fall our little wooden dock would faithfully keep watch over boats, fishing poles, inner tubes, and my homemade mud pies. Many people walked that dock over the twenty some years that we lived there. I loved our little castle on the lake, the dock, the beach, the seasons, and all the memories that were attached.

Mom and Dad had three boys before their first baby girl was born, me. I was crowned *Princess* right from birth. I was the lone holder of that title for almost five years before my sister Lori was born. I gladly shared my crown with her. As little girls we would play our version of "*Princess*" down on the wooden dock. Our imaginations would transform ordinary beach towels into locks of honey-spun *Princess* hair adorned with golden crowns. Additional transformed towels were used to cover our swimsuits and make evening gowns with long, flowing trains.

Once adorned, we would "walk the dock." The dock was our pretend runway, where we could show off our sparkly clothes to the royal subjects who anxiously awaited our grand march. There really were not any royal subjects to speak of, just the sunfish that lived under the narrow wooden dock. Yet, we would carefully watch our step, so we would not trip, or worse yet, fall into the shallow water and join our admirers. As far as we were concerned, we were in our own little world—playing *Princess.*

We would mimic the beauty queens on television. One at a time we would slowly walk down to the end of our makeshift runway and give a gentle back-and-forth wave of the wrist. We had a "no armpit exposure" rule on our runway. A graceful pivot turn would head us back up to dry land. This make-believe *Princess* thing, along with the making of mud pies and sandcastles, occupied most of our daily play routine for many summers as little girls.

Back then, playing *Princess* was only an imaginary child-like fantasy to me. Being a royal daughter of some King was a high and lofty thing to which only the blood-born privileged could attain. Never in my wildest dreams did I ever imagine this would happen to me in real life. Can you believe it did? The high calling of being a *Princess* in a very real kingdom—the kingdom of God—came knocking at my door. I opened the door and answered the call from my heavenly Father. The dock I now walk on is made of heavenly matter and is leading me to my eternal destiny. He made this dock just for me, and He has also made one just for you.

We all have to travel down the dock of life one way or another. So why not do it as royalty? There is no better way than as the daughter of the Most High King. If you let Him, He will adorn you with beautiful garments, crown you with eternal salvation, and walk with you down your life's wooden dock. Our King and Father promises to never leave us or forsake us. We will never walk it alone. When the King gives His Word, it cannot be taken back, and you can bank on it being true.

Childhood Memories Linger Long

I was raised in a large mainstream denominational church. This may sound funny, but I remember feeling sorry for all the people that were not part of my denomination. I really believed they would not make it into heaven. I find it interesting that at such a young age I had already formed the opinion that my denomination was the only way into the kingdom of Heaven. At this point in my life I obviously did not understand what the kingdom of God was all about.

My elementary education was at a private school. Certain memories stand out in those school days. I remember in first grade watching my classmate cry when she woke up from naptime and found she had wet her pants. That was confusing. Second grade was the year I memorized the song, "As I Go A-Wandering." That was fun. In third grade, Tommy M. decided he was in love with me and bought me stuffed animals, rings, and candy. That was silly. Fourth grade marked the year I was finally tall enough to get the next size school uniform. This also meant that I could finally reach the water fountain without the little stepstool that Barney our janitor had made for me in first grade. That was a milestone.

Fourth grade also brings back bad memories of an arithmetic teacher. One day in front of the whole class she said something like, "Robin, you're being lazy and stupid." I hated math from that point on because I believed that lie. That one comment stayed with me until I was an adult. That was heartache.

In fifth grade my shiny red clogs made quite a statement against the boring colors of our uniforms. That was planned. I also had a male teacher for the first time in my educational experience. That was interesting. And I forever hold a picture in my mind of my friend Nancy barfing in front of the whole class. It was gross.

In sixth grade I went through a best friend crisis. I also memorized the Ten Commandments. Sadly, I also remember being asked to sing at a funeral of a Senior High student who crashed his motorcycle and died. Death became real to me that day. That was eye-opening.

GOT RELIGION OR RELATIONSHIP?

Religion class was always part of that private school curriculum. We learned prayers and Bible stories and were taught about our denomination. This is where I was taught about God the Father, Jesus the Son, and the Holy Ghost. At this point in my life I did not have any revelation of being a *Princess,* let alone a daughter of the Most High God. I had head knowledge of God, but it had not quite hit my heart that He was the Father.

Of the many different Bible stories we were taught, I especially remember the story of Adam and Eve, the first people God made on earth in the Garden of Eden. I think I remember this one so well because I hate snakes! Here is my summary of the story, it is pretty much a 1–2–3 kind of deal.

1. God created the first man from the dust of the earth; breathed life into him and named him Adam. Adam was made in God's own image. All the animals were created and God gave Adam the privilege of naming them. I always wondered how he remembered all the names once he named them.

2. God saw that Adam needed a helpmate, probably to help him remember all the animals' names. Just kidding. God just knew Adam needed a companion. God put Adam to sleep and took out the female portion that was within him to create woman. I wondered if it hurt when the bone came out. Adam named her Eve. Adam and Eve lived in the Garden and walked with God daily. They had an awesome relationship with God and each other.

3. One-day God's enemy, the devil, disguised himself as a snake. He talked Eve into eating fruit from a tree that God forbade them to touch. She not only ate, but also gave some to Adam. Their relationship with God was never the same after that famous bite of the forbidden fruit of the Garden. This sin separated mankind from God.

End of story, my nutshell version anyway. It seemed like an interesting enough Bible story at the time. However, this story was not life changing news to me. I could hardly believe that Adam and Eve would listen to a snake. Since when did snakes talk? Not to mention that this seemed like no ordinary snake. He was filling their ears with nice talk, but deceiving their hearts with evil. I could never picture myself buying a lie from some fork-tongued reptile.

At the ripe old age of eleven I figured I was safe in the God department. My head knowledge seemed like it was enough. I never thought of myself as a sinner like Adam and Eve. They seemed to have really blown it with God. I thought going to church excluded me from being a sinner. Like I said before, I believed I was going to heaven because I was a member of a large denominational organization.

I did not have the understanding of being a *Princess* in an eternal Kingdom.

Outside of religion class, I never read the Bible. We had one family Bible in our home that was kept on the living room shelf. It was one of these extremely gigantic leather Bibles that takes two people to carry. My sister and I would read the names of all the people in our family tree inside the front cover. All sorts of interesting family facts were documented on the front page: dates of marriages, births, childhood diseases, and deaths in the family. That was the extent of my Bible reading. I did not think I needed to read the Bible. That job belonged to the guy at church.

As far as going to a church service, we would go almost every Sunday and definitely holidays. Holiday services were my favorite because they were always different from the weekly services. Many more people would come to the services and the building would usually be decorated to match the holiday.

I had a favorite place to sit in the church building during the service. It was on the left side, in the middle. I liked sitting on the end of the pew by the aisle. That way, as the people would line up to take Communion, I could look at all the ladies' shoes as they passed by. Funny, I still love looking at shoes. I remember hearing someone say, "You can tell a lot about people by the shoes they wear." I have remembered that quote through the years. I often wonder how accurate that quote is.

This final little story I do not personally remember, but it was passed down as one of those never-to-be-forgotten moments in my history. My mom would rather it be forgotten; but oddly enough, it is fitting for this book.

This little incident took place when I was only two years old. It was my brother Billy's job to get me dressed for church service that particular Sunday morning. Mom set out a fluffy dress, lacey socks, and shiny shoes. Everyone in our family appeared just fine that morning as we darted off to the service.

This church had long wooden pews in which the congregation would sit. Our family sat down in "our pew." It was not really "our pew," but we always seemed to pick the same spot to sit just like everyone else in the church. Well, being the inquisitive two-year-old that I was, I leaned over the pew in front of ours. I was probably trying to see if anything more exciting was happening up there. It was while I was leaning over, however, that my mother made the amazing and horrifying discovery that I had no undies on! There I was hanging over the pew in front of God and the whole church family with no underwear! How embarrassing for my mom! And a major bummer for Billy—bare butt and all, I was a *Princess*-in-the making back then and did not even know it.

Looking back at my childhood, I have many warm and loving memories. I was loved and cared for by my family. Even though religion was a big part of our lives, I did not have a personal relationship with God the Father, Jesus His Son, or the Holy Spirit. I was definitely a *Princess* in my parent's kingdom, but not yet a *Princess* in my heavenly Father's Kingdom.

Personal Princess Reflections

1. List some of your favorite memories from when you were little.
2. Does your Mom/Dad/Guardian have any favorite sayings that you remember? Are they true?
3. Do you think you receive a free ticket to heaven because you belong to a certain church? Do you think it matters what church you attend?

4. Have Bible stories made an impact on your life? If so, which ones? If not, why?
5. When you think back on your early childhood, what do you picture? Joy, happiness, sadness, anger, a mixture?
6. What thought was most significant to you in this chapter?

Chapter 2

The First Royal Family

I AM NOT THE only one who had an underwear issue in the past. Adam and Eve had a thing about underwear. You can read all about it in Genesis 3. I would like to expand on their particular underwear story.

You could say that Adam and Eve were the first royal family on earth. Adam's name means "man of red earth." Eve's name means "life-giver."[1] When God made Adam and Eve, He gave them the Garden of Eden to inhabit. Whoa, what a piece of property to inherit! They had everything they needed right there in the Garden. They lived in a glorious kingdom, tailor made by God for them to enjoy. It was awesome! God would talk with them every day whenever they wanted. He loved His creation and His creation loved Him.

God's Glory Covering

The Bible says that God's very own glory *covered* Adam and Eve. His glory was just like royal robes of clothing to them. Have you ever seen pictures of Adam and Eve with clothes on? I never have. They are usually standing behind a big bush or tree; you can tell they have nothing on. That is because they were naked and were created to have no need of clothing. They had no need of undies, or fancy shoes! The glory of God covered them. That was true until the devil came around and deceived them. Remember the forked-tongued snake?

There were two special trees in Eden. The first was called "the tree of life," and the other was "the tree of the knowledge of good and evil." God instructed Adam and Eve not to eat from the second tree. God specifically told Adam that if he ate from it he would die. God's instruction was crystal clear.

It appears from the story that Adam and Eve never even thought about that particular tree or its fruit until the day the devil slipped into the picture. Disguised as a snake, the devil began to deceive Eve with crafty words. He told her she could be like God if she ate the fruit from the tree of good and evil. Can you just picture the forked tongue in his mouth spewing out crafty words? He needed to be crafty because Adam and Eve were already made in the image of God. Why did they need to be any more like Him? They were already the closest thing to what God could make in His image. God did not make rejects. They were perfectly created in God's image. In Genesis 1:26, it says, "Then God said, 'Let Us make man in Our image, according to Our likeness'...." Who are the "Us" in this passage? Father, Son, and Holy Spirit. They are the Godhead, better known as the Trinity.

LIAR, LIAR PANTS ON FIRE

So how did Eve fall for his trick? Here is the deal. The devil also knew about the free will that was given to the first royal family. They could make choices while on earth. Up to this point they always chose God and His ways because of the relationship they had with Him. There was no reason to choose differently; life in the garden was awesome. Satan knew he had to use their free will somehow to thwart God's plan for a human race that loved and worshipped God. So, he did what he does best—he took a truth and twisted it. Typical liar.

Eve heard the snake say, "If you eat the fruit from this tree you will be like God..." (Gen. 3:4, author's paraphrase and emphasis). Her heart was to be like God, because she totally loved Him and thought, "Wow! What an opportunity to really be like Him!" So you see, Satan's deceit was used as his twisted words pierced Eve's heart. She fell for the line and ate the piece of fruit. The devil does not always come as a big, mean, ugly, red-faced monster twisting your arm until you say, "Uncle." He can make anything sound good, righteous, and even godly. But it can be so wrong! Instead of obeying God and leaving that fruit tree alone, Eve listened to the lies of the devil. Have you ever done that? It is easy to do. She even talked Adam into eating from that fruit tree. Why not? They were going to be more like God if they did. Right?

The Beginning of the End

That was the beginning of the end for Adam and Eve. Once they disobeyed and ate the fruit, they immediately could feel the change in their relationship to God their Father. Their perfect kingdom in the Garden was forever changed. That was exactly what the devil had in mind. Their choice caused a rift in their once perfect relationship to the Father.

Romans 6:23 says, "For the wages of sin is death." A wage is a payment you receive for something you do. The payment for their disobedience was death. A spiritual death set in immediately; physical death came years later. God's covering of glory left them.

God and sin do not mix. You see, sin separates us from God. Without God we are spiritually dead, doomed to eternal damnation. This was not God's original plan for the royal couple! They were supposed to live in His glory for eternity!

Genesis 3:7 says, "Then the eyes of both of them were opened, and they knew they were naked." Although they had no clothes on before they disobeyed, they still had the glory covering them. Once the glory left they saw they were naked. This is saying that the result of the first sin was self-centeredness. All of a sudden they were worried about themselves.

Before they sinned, Adam and Eve did not even know how to be self-centered. All Eve wanted to do was be more like God. How did all this happen? They only knew how to be God-centered before this big mess. They had no worries before they sinned; suddenly they only worried about themselves. What a change! No wonder they ran and hid!

FIG LEAF UNDERWEAR

Now they "saw" their nakedness and ran to hide from God. Yeah right—like you can hide from God! So there they were, with no glory covering them, and hiding from God. What did they do? They made fig leaf underwear! Yep, that is right, underwear! Not quite like the cotton ones we wear today. They gathered leaves off of a nearby fig tree and somehow designed undies. The scratchy kind.

When my husband and I went to Israel, we saw many fig trees. The leaves on those trees are very large. This story makes even more sense to me as to why they chose the leaves of the fig tree. I guess that would have been my first choice in underwear.

So why did they make undies? I believe it is because underwear covers a very private part of our body. The word private means "not publicly or generally known, confidential." Think about it. It is symbolic. Like Adam and Eve, we try to hide our private thoughts and sins from God. We think our thoughts and actions are confidential, as if God cannot see them. We try and keep our sins hidden from others and God. Adam and Eve tried using these fig leaf undies to hide from their sin. We use other things like lies, exaggerations, justifications, and excuses. They are just like the fig leaves Adam and Eve used to make undies. You cannot hide from God Almighty. He sees and knows everything about us every day, every minute, and every second.

Self-Centeredness Originated in the Garden

We *all* think our sins are hidden before we really know the King of Kings. Ever since Adam and Eve began this sin thing, we all have fallen short of God's glory and have tried to cover up with fig leaves. We too put fig leaves over ourselves—our hearts—to try and hide the sin. We put these leaves on without even knowing it. Nevertheless, God still sees through *all* our fig leaves, just as He did Adam and Eve's. Our inheritance, like it or not, from Adam and Eve, the first royal family, was the sin of self-centeredness.

The Father in His great mercy calls out to us by name, as He did Adam and Eve when they were hiding in their new undies. In Genesis 3:9 it says, "Then the Lord God called out to Adam and said to him, where are you?" (emphasis added). Now do you think for a moment that God Almighty had to ask Adam where he was? No! But God knew that by calling Adam by his name, and asking him where he was and why he was hiding, He could possibly get Adam to confess his sin of disobedience. Confession of sin is the beginning of restoring our relationship back to the Father. God made Adam take responsibility for his action.

However, when God asked Adam where he was and why he was hiding, He did not get the confession of the sin He was expecting. Adam answered back to God and even blamed the woman, which God had given him. This effectively put the blame back on God for his sin, because it was God that made the woman. Then the woman blamed the snake for her sin of disobedience. Since God allowed the snake in the Garden, it must be God's entire fault, thereby effectively putting the blame back on God. How convenient. This however, was definitely the wrong answer!

BLAMING OTHERS ORIGINATED IN THE GARDEN

As you can see, we not only inherited the sin of self-centeredness from the first royal family, but also the sin of blaming others. These two inherited fig leaves are the reasons we create lies, exaggerations, excuses, and justifications. The longer they sit on our hearts, the harder they are to peel off. The only solution to soften these hard fig leaves is His love.

WHEN I BECAME PART OF THIS ROYAL FAMILY

My life relates to the story of Adam and Eve. It was all part of the making of this *Princess.* God the Father knew where I was, called my name, and came to me. I did not even realize I was hiding from Him until I heard Him calling my name. No, I was not naked and standing behind a bush with fig leaf undies on like Adam and Eve. I had the fig leaf undies on my heart.

When I was fourteen years old, my parents sent me to a Christian summer camp in North Carolina called "Young Life." The year was 1978. It was the week before the Fourth of July. My parents knew I would hear the message of God's kingdom while there. It was important to them for me to hear it. They had just become part of this royal family of God and somehow knew it was just what their little *princess* needed. I just thought I was going for the horseback riding, waterslides, and swimming pools that were in the brochure! I did not care what they called the camp; it looked exciting!

My Insecurities

Packing for camp, I brought along my brown polka dot swimsuit, white tube top dress, hiking boots, jean shorts, tank tops, undies, blow dryer, cigarettes, and two joints (marijuana). Those last two items were packed just in case I needed to try and fit in with new friends. They are called false securities. Surprised? Don't be. I would sometimes use these false securities to secure my cool group status. With camp, I did not know what to expect, and I definitely wanted to fit into the cool group there. That was my life mission.

Most girls have something they use to help them fit in, or in other words feel accepted. Maybe you use make-up, money, clothes, friendships, alcohol/drugs, intelligence, or whatever. It is anything you use to help you feel secure. Somewhere I got the stupid idea that these cigarettes and joints made me look more mature. So, in my mind, I thought if I looked mature, the other kids could not mark me as insecure. For some reason, I thought insecure people were not cool. Therefore, I needed to feel accepted and popular in order to be secure about myself. So whatever it took to fit in at camp with the cool group, I was prepared to face.

These insecurities about who I was ended up being one of the reasons I tried drugs and alcohol. Fear of the possible rejection from those I deemed popular kept me feeling like I needed to be exciting and mature. Interesting items I picked out to be exciting and mature, eh? What a joke! These items will actually work the opposite in your life. I obviously did not know that at the time.

The turmoil at home created some of the insecurity I was feeling. However, these insecurities were mainly due to a childhood memory that had a big fat lie attached to it. I actually believed I was stupid and not worth anything. Now, you are asking, "How in the world does that happen to a girl that was raised in a loving family that gave her high self esteem and confidence right from her birth?" Read on!

Like most teenagers, I too was always looking for acceptance from others; to feel like I fit in, especially when I was put into a situation like camp where I did not know many kids. To find the cool group and belong was my first priority.

I do not want you to get the wrong picture here; I was not a big drug user. Actually I was a popular girl at school, into cheerleading, gymnastics, and drama. In some areas of my life I was secure and knew who I was. Like most people, I was secure in the things I knew I was capable of doing well, but insecure in the areas I was least knowledgeable. How I dealt with my insecurities was the real issue. For me, the insecurities were what triggered the crutch of using alcohol, weed, and cigarettes. I hid behind them. That is why it was a false security.

So with all my stuff packed, I was off to camp! As I climbed on the bus I was clueless as to what was about to take place. I would not be that same person when I returned home one week later.

Let the Fun Begin

Camp was so loaded with fun during the day that nobody had much time to think about trying to fit in. That was actually a relief; I could be myself for the most part. Thankfully, Lisa, one of my favorite friends, was shipped off to camp, too. We were in the same bunkhouse, and in the same boat of not knowing many people. Lisa was a lot more secure about who she was. She never seemed to let peer pressure influence her. She was someone I admired. Thank God for these kinds of friends. The only time I would feel insecure was when there were boys around who I thought were cute. Sound familiar?

The first night at camp the staff and campers crammed into a big, cozy room with shag carpet. After we all found our spot on the floor, we started singing charged up songs about God, life, and love. A few love ballads were sung, and then we were introduced to the staff. After introductions, a couple of the college-age staff volunteers got up on the stage and talked about their life with God. They did not seem a bit scared or embarrassed to talk about their faith in front of us. That impressed me. It was a perfect end to a great day. This was a ritual every night thereafter.

By mid-week, I noticed all of the staff at the camp seemed to know God in this special way. It bothered me that I did not know Him like they did. Even the way that they prayed and thanked God for the food at meal times got my attention. They did not pray the memorized version I had learned as a child. Their prayers were from the heart, as if they were actually talking to God right there! I remember thinking, "I want to pray like that."

By the third night I began to notice how the music

would speak to my heart in a way that made me feel loved, wanted, and cared for by God. I had never sung these particular songs before. Long after the lights were out for the evening, the words and music swirled around in my head while I laid on my bunk. I wondered why this music was affecting me. Actually, I was feeling infected by some unknown virus called love. The ultimate fig leaf dissolver.

A couple of the songs pounded out loud and clear, over and over. They left me with questions. Why do these words mean so much to me? I could feel the words penetrate my very being. I was beginning to feel a love that made me want to dance, shout, and sing. Somehow I was feeling freer as the nights went on.

These heartfelt worship songs made me want to meet Him face to face. I only knew of a God that sat on a throne with a whip ready to punish people who were bad. This Father was clearly not the same one! I wanted Him to be everything to me.

I was amazed at how each night the music would somehow magically prepare our ears for the camp speaker. One night, one of the counselors unfolded for us this mystery of Jesus Christ and who He was, and is, and is to come. This particular night the speaker shared with us how Jesus made it possible to know the Father. He told us that after the disobedience of Adam and Eve, God sent His own Son Jesus to save all of mankind from the consequences of sin. By living a perfect life, and taking the punishment we deserved for our sin, Jesus restored our relationship with the Father. Without it, we were doomed to eternal separation from Him. Eternal separation is called hell. Hell is described in the Bible as a lake of fire that never goes out. This got my attention. (See Matthew 18:9.)

This man Jesus started to become real to me; He was no longer just a story in the Bible. It never occurred to me until that very night that He came to earth, died, and rose again for me to have fellowship with the Father. Why would someone die for me? As I listened to the camp speaker, I saw and knew it was all about love. The Father loved me! Jesus loved me! I was extravagantly loved!

This was life-changing news to me. His perfect love was casting out my fears. His love was becoming my ultimate security blanket. The amount of love I was experiencing from the Father was overtaking me. And yet the whole idea of being a sinner and needing a savior was hitting my heartstrings and playing a tune I had never heard. I felt like I was being drawn towards something warm and deep, yet somehow painful. This was a new experience for me. What was this feeling? Was this true love?

I began to see that I was a sinner just like Adam and Eve, and that I, too, needed to be redeemed from this curse of separation from God. I began to see the fig leaf undies on my heart!

Until this time, I never considered myself a sinner. This was where the pain was coming from. The light went on. God the Father sent His own Son, Jesus, to bring us back into right relationship again with Him. Jesus was obedient to His Father's will of coming to earth, to die, and give all of mankind the opportunity to be saved.

Whoa, what a love story! It all made sense. It was all so simple. My heart was pounding in anticipation of speaking face to face with the Father. Here was my opportunity to meet him face to face just like the song we were singing each night.

Would He really accept me into this royal family and walk beside me day by day? How do I do this? Where do I find Him? The camp director said we could have that assurance of salvation and the Fathers love tonight if we wanted it. We just needed to ask for it.

THE KING FINDS ANOTHER PRINCESS

All of the campers were challenged to go out after the meeting ended to find a quiet place alone and talk to God about our relationship with Him. My heart continued its anxious pounding as I climbed a small hill and found my spot in the dark starry night. Looking up at the stars through streams of tears pouring from my eyes, I wondered how I possibly could express with words what I was feeling inside. I humbly spoke out, "God, I want to know you like these people seem to know you." Right then I sensed an overwhelming wave of His love flood over me. I knew He heard me crying out to Him. I felt like Adam and Eve in the garden. I could almost hear Him saying, "Robin, I love you. Where are you and why have you hidden from me?" I spoke back to Him that I was ashamed of my sin. I told Him I needed Him in my life.

I could hardly stand seeing my sin. I could relate to the feeling of nakedness Adam and Eve experienced. I could see my need of clothing (salvation from sin) before the Father. It was so painful. I saw that Jesus was made to be that clothing. I asked Jesus to rescue me, and He did. The warmth and depth of this moment will never be forgotten. I cried so hard that I felt as if my guts were going to explode and my heart burst. I could hardly process the love that was being poured into me.

Jesus purchased this glory covering for me by dying on the cross. His very own blood paid for all of my sin and for my covering. I went from fig leaves to glory! My camp counselor, Joanne, found me as I was making my way back to the cabin. I told her what happened to me on the hill and she prayed with me. Standing on the cabin steps, I cried in her arms because of the relief of finding a Savior, and the joy that was overflowing in me that night. She was just as excited as I, because she knew I found my Savior Jesus and met My heavenly Father in a real way. I was now His *Princess.*

THE PRINCESS JOURNEY BEGINS

My relationship with Lisa became even closer after this life-changing week at camp. Lisa's name means "consecrated to God." She too was consecrated to Him that week. Our lives were both changed during that incredible week in North Carolina. We were not the same girls who had boarded the bus ten days earlier. There was much to learn about this kingdom of God. The *Princess* journey had just begun.

It all made sense to me. What I thought was just a nice story at one time became a personal story of the love of God the Father, and His son Jesus. I became a daughter of the King of Kings and Lord of Lords. I became a real *Princess* of the Most High King. The next morning I could hardly wait to throw away all the false security items I brought to camp. I felt so free. So loved. I saw that those insecurity hang-ups were sin, and wanted nothing to do with them. I did not want to do anything that would hurt my relationship with my Father.

It felt so good to dump the cigs and pot in the garbage can. The King had accepted me, and I felt more secure with His love than with anything I had ever experienced in life. What more did I need? This alone was precious to me. At the time I felt as if I could conquer the world. Little did I know the challenges that were ahead of me.

YOU CAN BE A PRINCESS, TOO

We all have a big hole inside of us that can only be filled by the supernatural love of God. Have you ever wondered why so many people are reading about new age philosophies, witchcraft, and wizard spells? Maybe you have been one of them. Instead of seeking God, they go searching to find something to fill their emptiness. Only God the Father through Jesus can fill that void, bring peace, and the supernatural resurrection power of eternal life. No spell can match that power!

The hole inside of me was filled. I was now part of His royal family. Colossians 1:13 says, "He has delivered us from the power of darkness and conveyed us into the kingdom of the Son of His love." Wow! That happened to me, and it can happen to you!

You can become a *Princess* in the royal family of God—a real true-to-life *Princess*, daughter of the Most High King. He comes and knocks at the door of our hearts, and we have the free will to respond back to Him by opening that door and inviting Him in. God will take anyone who opens the door to Him. If you have never heard this message before, and want Jesus to come and restore you back to the Father, just ask Him! Open up that door.

You can do it right now, right here. This simple prayer will change your life. Just say…

> *Jesus, I want to be restored back to the Father, and be a Princess. Forgive me of my sins and take off my fig leaves. Come into my life, change me, and fill me with Your Holy Spirit.*

This is how my walk down the dock began as a *Princess*, daughter of the Most High King. You too can walk the runway—as a royal *Princess*!

PERSONAL PRINCESS REFLECTIONS

1. What is something you have done where you knew immediately when you did it that it was wrong and you were in trouble?

2. What went through your mind?

3. What did you think was going to happen?

4. Did you try and cover it up? How?

5. Did you try and make it right? Did it work?

6. What things do you do to try and fit in?

7. Are these things that you enjoy? Why or why not?

8. Are you part of this royal family of God? How do you know?

9. Describe how this chapter personally spoke to you.

Chapter 3

CINDERELLA: THE FICTIONAL PRINCESS

IT WOULD BE hard to find a little girl in America who does not know of the beautiful *Princess*, Cinderella, popularized by the Walt Disney film classic. Her story is ageless.[1]

Once upon a time, in a land far away, lived a beautiful young woman named Cinderella. She lived a life of luxury in a gigantic castle with her loving parents. Cinderella's life appeared complete, happy, and carefree. Have you ever met a real life Cinderella? They seem to have everything. Well, even what seems so ideal can change in a second.

Cinderella had one of those seconds. It all began on the dreadful day her mother passed away. She and her father were left to live in the beautiful castle alone. This death was a great loss to Cinderella and her father. The emptiness in the spacious castle and in their grieving hearts was too much to bear. Her father eventually found himself a new wife to try and fill the void.

The Original Step Monster

This new wife had two daughters of her own. They were all brought to the castle to live with Cinderella and her father. Soon after, tragedy struck again. Cinderella's father suddenly passed away. This is when Cinderella's circumstances changed from bad to worse. When her father died the stepmother (or should we say stepmonster) and stepsisters manifested every sort of evil against Cinderella. The stepmother began treating Cinderella like a slave. The root of this evil treatment was jealousy. She was jealous of Cinderella's beauty and grace, which caused her to treat Cinderella like dirt. Although Cinderella was trapped as a slave in her father's castle, she remained a loving and kind girl.

Her Redemption Was Near

A King lived in the same region as Cinderella. He had a son, Prince Charming, who needed a wife. So one day the King sent a decree from his palace. It said, "Hear ye, hear ye, hear ye, the King is searching the region for a *Princess* to be his son's bride. All the maidens in the region interested in meeting the prince are invited to a special ball."

Of course, the evil stepmother heard this and did not want the prince to get a look at Cinderella because of her beauty. Therefore, she made her stay home from the ball. This crushed Cinderella; she desperately wanted to go to the ball. Her chances of meeting the prince seemed low.

The Fairy Godmother Makes a Way

However, as the story continues, a certain fairy godmother (F.G.) drops by the castle. With a wave of the wand and a couple of funky words, Cinderella turns into a maiden fit for the ball. Without hesitation Cindy darted off to the ball in her private coach made from a pumpkin. She was adorned from head to toe with a golden crown, a drop-dead groovy gown, and sparkling glass slippers. F.G. said, "All things are possible to those that believe." What an awesome line!

Amazingly enough, Cinderella arrived just in time for the prince to glance at her from across the room. He was drawn to the beautiful maiden, gathered her into his arms, and twirled her around the dance floor. They instantly fell in love. Cinderella was so romantically swept off her feet she almost forgot about the agreement she had made with the F.G. before she left for the ball. Cinderella agreed to be back home by the stroke of midnight, at which time the coach and her elegant gown would disappear.

Therefore, at the first stroke of midnight, Cinderella pulled herself away from the arms of the prince and darted for her coach. As she ran down the palace steps, one of her glass slippers slipped off her foot. The prince could not understand why this beautiful maiden left his arms so quickly. His heart was broken. He did not even know her name or where she lived. He ran after her, but found only her glass slipper lying on the steps where it had fallen off her delicate foot.

What a story. No wonder every little girl loves this fairy tale! Even we big girls still love it!

THE SEARCH FOR CINDY WAS ON

In the morning, the love-struck prince set out to find his *Princess.* He was determined to find the owner of that glass slipper. It was the key that would lead him to his *Princess.* With the glass slipper in his hand, he searched throughout the kingdom for the one he loved whose foot would fit the slipper. He never stopped searching for his *Princess.*

The evil stepmother heard the prince's chariot approaching their castle. In an effort to keep the prince from getting a glance at Cinderella, she locked Cinderella in an upper room. From behind the door Cinderella heard the voice of her newfound love as she held the other glass slipper in her hand.

Locked in the Upper Room

In a last ditch effort to try and gain a royal *Princess* spot for one of her two daughters, the stepmother made her two daughters try and squish into the tiny glass slipper. However, the slipper was hand-made for only one girl, and would fit no other foot. The stepmother's attempt to outwit the prince was useless. Everyone knew that neither of the stepsisters was the beauty the prince had fallen in love with on the dance floor the previous night. The slipper proved it.

With the help of little mice and only seconds to spare, Cinderella broke free from behind the locked door. She ran to Prince Charming. Immediately the prince knew this girl was the fair maiden he had fallen in love with the night before. The glass slipper was a perfect fit. He carried her away from the bondage of the evil stepmother, and they lived happily ever after. What a dreamboat he was, and her savior from a life of bondage and punishment!

Our Princess Title Is Not a Fairy Tale

So how does this fictional story of Cinderella relate to us as *Princesses* of the Most High King? Unlike Cinderella, our title of *Princess* is not just a fairy tale; it is very much a reality.

To draw similarities and relate this story to our own lives we need to compare the wicked stepmother in this story to what we know of as "bondage." One of the meanings of the word bondage is slavery. Cinderella was treated as a slave by the wicked stepmother. This was a form of bondage to her. We too are born slaves to sin because of Adam and Eve's fall from grace in the Garden of Eden. We are held in bondage until Jesus, our Prince of Peace, frees us from being slaves of sin and death.

Like Cinderella we hear the King give the decree, "Hear ye, hear ye" from the kingdom of God. The King of the universe calls each and every one of us to come and meet His Son, the Prince of Peace. Hopefully we heed that invitation and go to the ball, meet Jesus, our Prince of Peace, and everything is beautiful, fresh, and new. My ball just happened to be in North Carolina on a hill!

When we meet the Prince of Peace our slavery to sin and death is washed away. Cinderella felt like this when the prince's eyes melted into hers on the dance floor. She knew that he was her deliverer from the evil stepmother. His love would bring her deliverance. The Father's love brings us deliverance too.

What an awesome night; she was finally saved. Cinderella was so happy dancing in the prince's arms at the ball, knowing she had found true love and true freedom from bondage. I too was dancing in my heart the night I met Jesus. I knew He was my answer to freedom from the bondage of sin and death.

THE STROKE OF MIDNIGHT

Cinderella knew when she heard the stroke of midnight she needed to return to her home. The sound of the clock striking midnight was a reminder to her that she was not yet totally free. Regardless of her meeting the Prince, she returned to bondage at home. She had tasted freedom and love for a brief moment. She forgot the words of the F.G., "All things are possible to them that believe." She could have believed in the Prince's love, instead of the lie that persuaded her to flee from love.

How does this relate to us? I too have hit the stroke of midnight since I met Jesus. When I met Jesus, I knew He was my deliverer; yet I still had locked doors in my life that held me in unknown bondage. The stroke of midnight hits all of us from time to time in our walk on the dock as a *Princess*. Bondages from our past try to keep us away from our newfound love, just like they did for Cinderella. These bondages are lies that need to be exposed. They will try to keep us from being free, just like having an old, evil stepmother around!

Have you ever felt like you have been thrown in a room and the door was locked behind you? This can be so frustrating because you know the Prince has set you free. You know that He is your deliverance from all the past. Yet there you are feeling stuck behind what seems to be a big locked door. This locked door will keep you from going forward on the dock of your destiny.

Unresolved Issues of the Past

We generally feel locked behind a door when we have failed to deal with our past. I am talking about those memories that you know are holding you back from your destiny. These are the memories that usually have lies attached to them. The lies, not the memory itself, are the culprits of this type of bondage. Emotions triggered in current circumstances of our lives often remind us of the emotions experienced with certain memories—good and bad. All our senses can trigger memories. To successfully go into your future and walk out your destiny you need to learn how to expose these lies. This is where watching your emotions come in handy!

Emotions are good and given to us by God. Certain emotions can actually help you link back to the very memory with the lie attached. Saying to yourself, "Why do I feel scared when I see that? Why does this person make me so angry? Why do I feel like vomiting when I think about this subject? Why do I feel shaky when this happens to me? Why does that smell bother me so much?" And the list of questions goes on, that you can ask yourself to determine the cause. But until this is done, you will remain right where the lie has you. Where? In bondage to that lie. Just like a slave.

Could Cinderella have possibly believed the lie that the Prince would not love her if she were changed back into an ordinary slave girl at midnight? Maybe. If so, this lie forced her back into slavery and put her behind a locked door. This lie kept her from going forward with her newfound love. You do not want that to happen with you and Jesus, your newfound love, either!

The prince seemed to prove the lie false. Cinderella was an ordinary maiden, a slave girl, when the prince finally found her at home. His feelings for her had nothing to do with the gown, crown, and shoes she wore the night before. She should have stayed at the ball and had a ball! He did not care what she wore. See how lies will steal from us?

IT IS TIME TO OPEN THOSE LOCKED DOORS

Did you know that the stroke of midnight is the darkest hour on the clock? Nevertheless, what comes right after the stroke of midnight? Morning! Once Cinderella met the Prince she was on the road to freedom. I say "on the road" because she still needed to deal with that bondage of the evil stepmother before she would be totally free.

We, too, meet Jesus our Prince, and immediately we are put on the road called freedom. This road offers us the opportunity to deal with our examples of bondage as they are being exposed, or we can continue to stay locked behind the door. It is always best to deal with them as soon as they are exposed. If we continue to hide behind them, they become all the more difficult to destroy.

Morning light was shed on the darkness that prevailed in the castle when Cinderella came out from behind the locked door. Once she slipped her foot into the slipper, her destiny was sealed. The truth that the glass slipper belonged to Cinderella was the light that dispelled the darkness.

Cinderella was finally free from what was keeping her from her prince. We, too, have doors that are holding us back from our Prince. Cinderella was not about to let a stepmother keep her from her love and freedom. When the old bondage tries to hold us back, it can be easier and sometimes more comfortable to hide behind the door instead of destroying it and being free. We need to be as aggressive as Cinderella! Fear of facing the lie can hold you back just as well.

Exposing the Lie Attached to the Memory

What do you do when you hear the stroke of midnight? In other words, what is the action you take when a situation triggers an old memory, and you once again hear the lie that is attached to it? Do you have a tendency to take the same action and run in fear like Cinderella?

So let's listen to your stroke of midnight. Could it be the fights with your brother or sister that make you so mad you want to scream, "I hate you!" Or maybe a friend got the promotion at work that you thought you should have gotten, and now you are so upset you cannot even look at them! Or how about not getting an invitation to the party that everyone else got invited to? Why is your button being pushed? Why do you feel like you do? What is motivating this emotion of hatred, upset, or rejection? Anyone can push your buttons. It can be coworkers, friends, teachers, drivers, neighbors, parents, bullies…you fill in the blank!

As a *Princess,* you have been told by God's very Word, the Bible, to repent when you act this way. And you probably do. This takes care of the immediate sin for that day, and this method may work for a time, but sooner or later you will end up with the same reaction because you have not dealt with the lie.

People learn different ways to cope with difficulties and circumstances in life. Maybe you have learned to blame others so you do not have to deal with the lies you believe about yourself. Or maybe you take on shame and condemnation because you cannot seem to get victory over that particular ungodly reaction. Should you just run and hide from people and circumstances? No, that is not the answer, either.

LET THE BUTTON PUSHING PEOPLE HELP!

I guarantee that in your life you will never run out of people who will bring out the worst in you. Really! Button pushing people are everywhere. When a button pusher pushes your button, and an ungodly reaction comes out, use it to your advantage! Simply ask the Lord to reveal why you reacted in that way. He can lead you back to a memory that has caused a locked door in your life. Running to Him is the answer. This is what will break the cycle of your reacting the same old way. The Lord will reveal the truth to you. You can rely on Him for that! He is faithful.

An old memory can be something as simple as being the last one chosen on a team during recess. I remember the humiliation of standing there all alone until the last name was called for baseball during Phys-Ed at school. No one wanted me on their team, because I was afraid of the ball! This was traumatic for me. I was used to being the popular girl and getting all the attention. This type of early childhood experience can create a locked door in your life. And that locked door would be called, Rejection. Then, as life goes on, every time you are not included, left out, or overlooked, you feel the pain all over again, just like you did when that door was locked the first time. Not only will you feel the familiar pain, but you will hear the familiar voice, and even begin to believe the lie it speaks about you. The lie will be something like, "Nobody will ever like you, because you are a loser."

Or maybe you have always struggled with your weight and have had to live through all the teasing and name-calling associated with that. Self Hatred could easily be the sign on that locked door. Even something like an accident in which you or others were badly hurt could cause a locked door of Fear.

There are many different sign names. Thank God for the opportunities that come our way to get free from them all! No matter what the name is on your locked door, you can be sure that Jesus is the key to open it up and set you free. I think you will find it interesting that being hurt or wounded can help you pinpoint a locked door. This is especially true if you begin to hear the familiar voice speaking the familiar lie. How?

Well, those lies are just like an activation system on your telephone. Every time your feelings get hurt or your button gets pushed, you begin to hear the same old lie. The hurt activates the voice that tells you the lie. It is a pattern. It is simple to recognize because it is always the same old stupid lie! Learning to recognize the pattern will enable you to find the locked door, tear down the sign, and expose the lie.

HERE IS A GOOD EXAMPLE

I never realized that a locked door called *Fear of Death* lurked inside of me from a bad auto accident I was in with my two daughters. I did, however, notice myself tightening up and clinching my teeth every time I crossed an intersection in a car after the trauma. At first I did not really pay much attention to it. I guess at that point I did not realize fear was the culprit. I thought I was just being more careful. Then it was exposed.

About one year after the accident I was on a ministry trip. Our ministry team was picked up at an airport by some friends. I thought the driver was driving unusually fast for the winter conditions outside, and I found myself in a panic. All I could think about was my accident. The lie I kept hearing was, "You are going to die." My teeth and jaw were clinched so tight they hurt.

I looked at my girlfriend and told her that I was in total fear of getting in an accident. Tears began to roll down my face. She recognized the fear and knew right off that it was from the car accident one year prior. She was right. So she exposed that locked door and prayed for me to be free from its bondage and it was gone. I asked the Lord to forgive me for hiding behind that fear of death and not trusting Him with my life. I had no idea it was there!

Now the lie of dying in a car crash could no longer work on me because it no longer had a locked door to hide behind! Once free, I began laughing and was fine the rest of the road trip. And we arrived safe. I no longer get stressed out at intersections either.

Sometimes the Lord will provide a good friend to help you. And sometimes you do it all on your own. He knows just what you need and when you need it.

The King Sees the Locked Doors

You might not be able to see every locked door in your heart, but God the Father sees them. His mercy allows situations and people to cross our path so we can be free! I feel as though he orchestrated the winter storm and the fast driver just to get me free from the *Fear of Death.* The truth is you are loved, accepted, cared for, and have a place in the Kingdom of God! You can have complete victory to live as a true *Princess.* So go ahead and let the button pusher people and circumstances lead you to freedom!

Another Locked Door in My Life

When I was a little girl a relative that was a young man took advantage of me in the wrong way. He abused me sexually. Maybe you have had a similar experience with sexual abuse or know someone that has. Abuse is everywhere in this world. Physical, emotional, verbal, and sexual abuse will always bring damage to a life. Being a minister I am not ignorant of the many cases of abuse. This is my story…

I remember believing the lie that I would get in trouble if anyone ever found out about the sexual abuse. At the time I did not know it was abuse. I just thought I did something wrong. As I grew older, whenever I felt shameful, fearful, or confused from any given situation, I was brought back to that memory. The lie I happened to believe was that I deserved to feel that way because of being a dirty little girl, with a dirty secret. Getting yelled at by a teacher, or being caught doing something wrong would set off the same old tape of lies that began playing way back when I was little. The lies I heard would say, "You should have, and could have, prevented that. You are a bad person. It is entirely your fault. You asked for it. You are a dirty little girl that has a dirty little secret."

Sexual abuse was an enormous locked door in my life. Shame, fear, and confusion all had their own locked doors as well. They were a bit smaller, but a locked door is a locked door. It was almost like it was their job to be the body guards and make sure the sexual abuse door remained locked up tight. This way I would never get free. What a setup. They tried to keep me in bondage so my life would be tainted and messed up. It is hard to rise above when you are being pressed down.

This is precisely the idea behind the devil's plan of attack. Can you see the bondage that the devil made in my life at such an early age? The memory of this abuse caused me to feel shameful about myself in many ways. I continually hoped it would just go away. I thought the whole mess in my mind would disappear by ignoring it, but it would not leave me alone.

By the age of fifteen I still had this secret of sexual abuse hidden in me. I never told anyone. I loved Jesus and was so thankful for Him, but I thought that this area was too painful and dirty to let Him in. For me to go back to that memory was almost like death. I was used to shame, fear, and confusion showing up with their lies anytime a friend or foe would hurt me physically, emotionally, or verbally. I did not know that they were all lies trying to keep me in bondage!

My Princess Destiny Was at Stake

My heavenly Father wanted me to walk the dock of my destiny in complete freedom. I did not understand that I was being held captive. We can only understand as much as we have been taught. Although I did not understand this revelation, it did not stop the Lord from doing what He was sent to do! He came to set the captives free. He sees the devil and his evil plans that are devised to steal, kill, and destroy the children of God. I am here to tell you that you can trust the Lord to help free you in every area of your life, too. Jesus is the Way, the truth, and the life. He is our Prince of Peace.

Cinderella knew the Prince was on his way to free her. Even the cruel stepmother knew the prince was on his way. The fight to try and keep Cinderella in bondage was great. Don't think the devil will not put up a fight to try and keep you in bondage, too. This is his ultimate goal. But even greater is the goal of our Father to have His Son Jesus set us free!

The Root of My Insecurity

As a little girl I just thought I would have to live with this secret the rest of my life. I learned how to hide it deeper and deeper. I pretended it was gone. This is dangerous. I am so thankful the Father knew it was there all along and He had an appointed time to set me free. Pretending something is not there does not make it go away, and when it remains it takes root, just like a weed. The longer a root remains, the deeper it goes, and the harder it is to pull out.

If you have ever pulled a weed out of the ground and studied the root, you will see many little attached roots growing out of the main one. The main root in me was sexual abuse. The smaller roots attached to it were shame, fear, and confusion. Eventually roots produce a plant that pops up in the earth and yields fruit. Insecurity was the fruit that constantly popped up in my life. It was evident in my spirit, soul, and body. The funny thing is that this insecurity issue was not always evident to others. I learned how to hide it well.

I GAVE HIM MY HEART, BUT NOT QUITE MY LIFE

I received a glimpse of the Father's freedom and security when I gave my heart to Him at camp. That was what compelled me to dump all my false securities into the garbage can. Cinderella felt the same way when she was at the ball with the prince and he was looking in her eyes. Everything was alive and full. Then at the stroke of midnight she had to leave him and go back to the castle and bondage. I too had to board the bus and go home to reality.

I had no idea that destroying locked doors from my past was part of God's plan for my future. I gave Him my heart, but not quite my life. I found out rather quickly after I was home from camp that the root of insecurity was still there. It kept me doing some of the same things I had wanted to stop doing.

The root of insecurity was loosened at my salvation; which is why I was beginning to feel secure and loved in a whole new way. Rain has the same effect on the dirt in a garden. It is always easier to weed a garden after a rainfall. His love for me was like rain on my heart, put there to help break up the hard dry ground so the root would come out easier in the near future. Our Father God is so loving, kind, gentle, patient, and forgiving.

During this season of my life I often felt as if I had lost my salvation because I would go back and forth from using my false securities. That made me sad, because I loved this new relationship I had found in Him, and using false securities made me feel far away from Him. I felt trapped. I did not realize condemnation was bombarding me with shame, fear, and confusion. They were screaming in my ear the same old refrain I heard as a child. Only now the lies I heard added God into the mix saying things like, "God thinks you are stupid and you will never be a good Christian... You're too dirty to be loved.... You need to try harder to be holy." Little did I know that the Prince was on His way! Are you seeing things that have taken root in your life, and are now producing bad fruit? Well, fear not! The Prince is on His way!

EXPOSING THE ROOT TO LIGHT UNLOCKED THE DOOR

The prince came looking for me! He said, "Enough is enough! Where is my *Princess*?" He had a glass slipper just waiting for me to slip on so I could continue my walk down the dock with Him.

At the age of fifteen and home again for summer vacation, Mom and I went to hear a Christian woman give her testimony about what God had done in her life. Her name was Pam Chall—I will never forget her. I thank God for the anointing on her that day. This woman's testimony was a key that the King used to open that locked door of bondage for this *Princess*.

Remember I told you I just hid the secret deep down in my heart hoping it would eventually go away? Well, as Pam began to share her life story with us, that hidden root of sexual abuse began to be uncovered. The locked door began to open and the bondage of that secret was being exposed.

As she spoke her testimony, my heart began pounding

so loud I thought others could hear it. She spoke about how God delivered her of eating disorders as a young girl. She also touched on sexual abuse. This is when I cringed...I cringed and could hardly breathe. I was wondering what was happening. I felt as if I were an audience of one. What I was hearing was hitting my heart.

Tears filled my eyes. I desperately wanted to tell my Mom about the abuse, but everything in me was choking my freedom to tell her. My Mother sensed something was wrong. She knew that whatever was causing me to feel this pain needed to be revealed. She asked me what was wrong and then asked me if I was ever hurt sexually at some time in my life. That was all I needed. I thank God for my Mom; she asked the right question.

THE TRUTH WON OVER DARKNESS

Just saying a simple, "Yes" to my Mother's question was all that was necessary for the rest to come pouring forth. I shared with my Mom how the relative had sexually hurt me when I was a little girl. I was sobbing as I spoke. Once the truth was exposed, the door swung open and somehow it was much easier to speak about it.

When a root of a plant is pulled out of the ground and exposed to light and air it is the beginning of the end for that plant. Most plant and tree roots have to stay covered to thrive. That is why they are underground and hidden in darkness and dirt. My childhood secret was no longer able to hide in the darkness.

After Mom and I talked, I talked to Pam. Pam and Mom both knew that deliverance was necessary to help bring healing to this situation. Deliverance is not scary or meant to be. Pam and Mom basically gathered a small group of women and began praying for me. They told sexual abuse to take a hike in the name of Jesus.

Shame, fear, and confusion were out of a job! It was like the hand of the Most High King pulled out the root of sexual abuse! Shame, fear, and confusion had nothing to hang onto anymore; they had to go with the root of abuse. They no longer could body guard something that was not there! Every locked door was opened.

I sensed such an overwhelming freedom when they were finished praying. I felt clean and pure beyond words. This *Princess* was free! Knowing Jesus understood and saw what happened to me was comforting. He did not like what happened either. His love healed me.

SAY "GOOD-BYE" TO THE LIES

When the lie you want to vanish is attached to a memory from an abusive situation, it is best to have someone help you that has understanding in this area of ministry. Ask the Lord for the right person (or persons) to be brought into your life. Seek counsel from mature believers that you trust about what steps to take for deliverance from lies created from your past.

A good indicator of needing outside help would be that the pain persists and you are not able to "pray" it away yourself. Deeper issues of bondage take Godly, anointed ministers that have knowledge and understanding of this type of ministry. God brought Pam along for me. He will help you, too! Do not be afraid to ask your pastors for help.

There may be other circumstances of life, which cause a lesser degree of pain, which you can handle on your own with prayer. Below is a sample approach for you to follow when you discover a locked door that seems to keep popping up. Use these steps as a guide to help you:

1. Pray and ask the Father, Son, and Holy Spirit for help. Rest in His presence.

2. Ask Jesus to reveal to you the memory with a lie attached that has made you run, hide, or act in an ungodly way.

3. Once the memory and lie are brought out into the open, ask Jesus to come in with His light of Truth to expose and expel the lies.

4. At this point, if necessary, you will need to forgive those who hurt you so Jesus can take away the pain. This light always exposes the darkness and opens our locked door. Learning to do this is our path to a life of freedom.

5. Ask the Lord for forgiveness if you have carried any ungodly thoughts or have committed any ungodly acts because of this situation.

6. Thank the Father, Son, and Holy Spirit for their help.

Your Memories will never go away, they are part of who we are. The pain that was attached is what goes away! Once you begin to understand this principle and how to appropriate it in your life you can also begin to help others. The past no longer has any power over your future.

OUR ROYAL CROWN, GOWN, AND SLIPPERS

True freedom came to Cinderella when she broke free from the locked door and slipped into her glass slipper held by her Prince Charming. The stepmother no longer had power over Cinderella. Off she went to be the new *Princess.* Once again she was adorned in her dazzling new gown, sparkling glass slippers, and a royal crown. Our salvation and freedom is not just a fairy tale!

Once you begin to understand who you are, as a child of the Most High King, there is nothing that can stop you from fulfilling your destiny. Just like the evil stepmother, as hard as she tried, even she could not stop the destiny of Cinderella.

WEAR YOUR CROWN PROUDLY

Your *Princess* crown is placed on your head when you begin this new life as a believer in Jesus. You are marked forever. Your crown is not one of earthly value like you would buy in a store. It is eternal and is your crown of salvation. Read the scriptures listed below:

1. "For the LORD takes delight in his people; He *crowns* the humble with salvation" (Ps. 149:4, NIV). Our crown represents the salvation the Father has given us through Jesus.

2. "Blessed is the man who endures temptation; for when he has been approved, he will receive the *crown* of life which the Lord has promised to those who love Him" (James 1:12). This is our eternal inheritance. The crown symbolizes the eternal life promised to us as His children of obedience. We obey the King because we love Him!

3. "...Everlasting joy shall be upon their heads" (Isa. 51:11, AMP). A joy crown for every believer! We can have this joy as we live on earth. We carry joy unspeakable because of who He is. Joy is part of the kingdom of God! This also applies to the joy we will have eternally in the heavenly kingdom that awaits us.

WEAR YOUR ROYAL GOWN WITH HUMILITY

Jesus, your Prince of Peace, also clothed you with a dazzling white robe of righteousness. You can find that in Isaiah 61:10 "...For He has clothed me with the garment of salvation". White robes denote salvation, purity, cleanliness, and joy. Jesus is your righteousness; His righteousness covers you just as a robe in the natural world covers your body. You do not need the F.G. to do the gown thing like she did for Cinderella. Jesus already did the gown thing!

The King, your Father, sees you in this royal robe. It sets you apart as His child and proclaims to Him that you are free from sin and death. You need to see yourself adorned in this robe, too. The more time you spend in the Presence of the Father, the clearer you will see your robe and just what it truly represents.

This robe was given to you when you began your walk as a *Princess.* You had a sin-soiled robe and Jesus bought you a new clean white one. Be quick to repent (change your way of thinking) and keep your robe clean before the King. Let His thoughts about you be your thoughts about you. Let the Truth set you free.

WEAR YOUR GLASS SLIPPER OF DESTINY BOLDLY

At the end of the Cinderella story, the Prince showed up with the glass slipper. Fitting into that slipper sealed Cinderella's destiny. Only the woman that fit the glass slipper could have the title of *Princess.* They were Cinderella's and hers alone. Can't you just imagine the word destiny etched into the side of those slippers?

Do you remember the one stepsister who tried to squeeze her oversized foot into the glass slipper? The stepsisters and stepmother wanted Cinderella's destiny. They knew whoever wore those glass slippers would receive the title of *Princess.* The devil will try hard to steal or smash your glass slipper, too! Do not let him send you crashing off the deep end of your dock. Your destiny is sealed in the blood of Jesus, and you are the *Princess,* daughter of the Most High King. Be bold and be strong.

No one else can fit into these special glass slippers made just for you. When you meet your Prince charming—Jesus—He places these glass slippers on your feet with His nail-scarred hands. As you slip into your glass slipper of destiny you begin to understand your eternal journey ahead with Him. Every step you take down the dock is a step closer to following Him on your way to eternity.

You can walk totally free in the destiny made just for you. All of the days of your life were written out before you were even yet formed in your mother's womb. Daily there are special plans and purposes to fulfill while you are on this earth. Your free will must say, "Yes" to His sovereign will.

So go for it! Do not be afraid to ask the King what it is He has in store for you. You have been freed from the bondage of sin. You are a *Princess,* daughter of the Most High King. Walk in that freedom in His glorious Kingdom with your head up and in confidence of your royal title!

Personal Princess Reflections

1. Is there anything in your life that makes you feel as though an angry stepmother has locked you in a room?

2. What is the lie or lies that are locking the door?

3. Do they have anything to do with physical or emotional abuse?

4. If you do not know what they are, ask yourself this question: Do I have a memory that can act as a road map to the locked doors that these lies live behind?

5. Are these lies now roots that are growing plants with bad fruit?

6. Can you identify and list the bad fruit you are seeing in your life from that root?

7. How can you let Jesus go with you to that memory, open the door, expose the lie, and heal the wound?

8. What good fruit do you see in others that attracts you to them?

9. What bad fruit do you see in others that causes you to run from them?

10. What fruit would you like to produce? Ask the Lord to help you. Pick out a scripture that will help you in this process.

11. How did this chapter affect you personally?

Chapter 4

What Does A Princess Look Like Anyway?

What does a *Princess* in the Kingdom of God physically look like? Well, just stop for a moment and go look in a mirror. Need I say more? There are many *Princesses,* and all are beautiful in the Father's sight. We are kind of like a large box of expensive, assorted chocolates. Everyone is different and unique. Our Father, the King of creation, has created each and every one of us for His good pleasure. As His special *Princess,* you are sweet, unique, and individual. Your outward beauty does not determine if you can have the title of *Princess* in His Kingdom. Judges do not select His daughters through some type of line up and beauty contest. The King chose you and He alone gave you the title of being His *Princess.* Your looks are just as unique as the destiny that has been created for you.

Your unique and special destiny unfolds before you as you walk the dock as the *Princess,* daughter of the Highest King. Everyday you are building your life in Him. Everything in your life works together for the good, including any dock injuries and wounds you may have acquired on the way!

When you love the Lord your God, and live according to His ways, He promises to take those hard things you have been through and turn them into good. Take note of the little word "if." The "if" makes it a conditional promise. You must do your part and live according to His ways and not to your own selfish desires. As you seek Him, each experience will build upon the last; He will not waste the smallest of opportunities to work on your behalf.

BEWARE OF THE DOCK PUSHERS

One summer day my little sister Lori was playing on the dock with the neighbor's granddaughter. She was very jealous of Lori and pushed her off the dock onto the sandy beach. This rage of jealousy gave Lori a trip to the emergency room and two-fractured collarbones. But a broken collarbone did not stop Lori from playing on that same dock the very next day. She forgave the little girl and went on.

We need to imitate this quick-to-forgive attitude that children so easily portray. Lori learned to be cautious around that particular little girl, and rightly so. We, too, will acquire wisdom for walking on our docks of destiny through trials and tribulation. You may very well get pushed off your dock, too. There will be dock injuries from time to time. Jesus Himself warned us of this. John 16:33 says, "In the world you will have tribulation; but be of good cheer, I have overcome the world." Nothing should stop you from walking the dock of your destiny.

The neighbor's granddaughter was not satisfied that day in being herself. She allowed her jealousy to cause injury to another. In a sense she was screaming, "I do not want to be a strawberry-nougat in this box of mixed chocolates, I want to be a chocolate covered-caramel like Lori!" That particular day she did not have the revelation of her uniqueness. It was evident in the jealousy that caused harm to Lori. The granddaughter surely needed someone to give her counsel to the lies in her life.

You too need this revelation of your uniqueness. The next Bible story will really help you see this simple truth that you are unique and you were created from head to toe, inside and out, for a specific purpose. Strawberry nougat and all! There is just no need to be jealous of others' looks or personalities. Nor is there any need to respond in an ungodly manner when hurt by someone who is jealous of you.

The Rachel and Leah Story

In the Book of Genesis you will find two unique individuals with two unique destinies to fulfill. They happened to be sisters and their names were Rachel and Leah. This Bible story clearly portrays that Leah was not a pretty gal, but Rachel, on the other hand, was very beautiful. What a lousy thing to be remembered for in the world's most famous history book! But even that had purpose in God's kingdom.

Imagine with me for a moment, falling in love with a very handsome man who came from a fairly wealthy family. This is not too hard to imagine! Now imagine you were engaged to this man of your dreams for seven years. Yes, I said seven years! Then finally the seven years are up and your wedding day comes, only to find out your father arranges your older sister to marry him instead of you! Now that is hard to imagine! Could that really happen? Read on and you will see. I will first give you the background of this story so you get the whole picture.

THE STORY BEGINS WITH JACOB AND ESAU

Jacob is the handsome guy in this Bible story. Jacob lived in Canaan with his parents Isaac and Rebekah and twin brother, Esau. When the boys were older, a major conflict between the two of them occurred. With the help of his dear ol' mom, Jacob tricked Esau out of his birthright. (His family inheritance as the firstborn son.) Naturally, Esau was enraged with Jacob when he figured out what happened. Their mother Rebekah overheard Esau vow to kill Jacob. So she worked fast on getting Jacob out of town and away from his livid brother. She talked Isaac into sending Jacob off to the land of Haran to choose a wife from the family of her brother Laban. This was all part of God's plan.

MAMA KNOWS BEST

Rebekah hoped that by sending Jacob to her brother's place in Haran, Esau would have time to cool off. She loved Jacob very much and did not want to see him killed by his twin brother. Uncle Laban was a landowner and sheepherder in this city. Laban had two daughters. Their names were Rachel and Leah.

JACOB MEETS RACHEL

When Jacob first arrived in the city of Haran, he met the beautiful Rachel at a well. She was about to give water to the flock of sheep she was tending. Coincidence? Never in God's kingdom! Jacob offered to water her flock for her, and then revealed his identity as her cousin from Canaan. He kissed her cheek, which was a typical thing for a relative to do. Rachel then brought him home to meet the rest of the family. Jacob met with her father, Laban.

Love at First Sight

At the well it was love at first sight for both Jacob and Rachel. Jacob knew immediately he wanted Rachel as his wife. Rachel was very young, but seemed to understand the feelings of love. It was quite typical in those days for cousins to marry. Families were large because the men had several wives.[1]

In the evening, Jacob met with Laban. He told Laban of his choice of Rachel as a wife. Laban agreed to give his daughter Rachel to Jacob in marriage, in exchange for seven years of work. Jacob agreed. A marriage contract was drawn, and everyone was happy. Soon after, Jacob began his new career in raising sheep and goats for Laban.

Jacob was so in love with Rachel that seven years seemed like a few days to him. Can you imagine seven years! When the seven years were up, Jacob went to Laban and asked for his promised *Princess.* It was time for the wedding feast and ceremony. Laban called all his friends together and threw a wedding party to fulfill the contract made to Jacob.

The Deceit of Laban

However, when it was evening, Laban sent Leah (Rachel's older sister) to Jacob's tent instead of Rachel. Jacob did not know this was Leah. Now, before you think this guy had no brains, you have to remember the time frame of history in which they lived. We are talking about no electricity in these tents made of dark goat's hair. There may have been only an oil lamp or a small fire for light. Leah was dressed as the bride, and probably had a veil over her face. I have a feeling that Leah was briefed by her father to speak as few words as possible so her voice did not reveal her identity. So this was the condition in which Jacob met Leah that night.

MY TENT-DWELLING EXPERIENCE

When my husband Chuck and I were in Israel we had the wild adventure of sleeping overnight in a real Bedouin tent just like Jacob's. We were taken to a camel ranch in the Negev Desert for this excursion. From the bus window, I saw a long, wide black tent and immediately looked at Chuck and said, "Take me back to the hotel!" My request was denied—I stayed. I managed to survive, and now can share my little tale with you.

The tent was really made from black goat's hair, just like Jacob's. Our bed mats were on the floor along with a type of sleeping bag. The stars in the sky were the only source of light after the bonfire dwindled down to cinders! We actually had electricity, but when the camp lights were shut off it was very, very dark. I can honestly attest to the fact of Jacobs's tent being pitch black.

THE LIGHT REVEALED THE TRUTH

The morning light appeared in the horizon when Jacob realized that it was Leah next to him in the tent and not Rachel. Immediately, Jacob went to Laban and protested. He was furious and asked Laban why he did such a thing. Laban said, "It is not permitted in our country to give the younger daughter in marriage before the eldest." Hello Laban! Seven years ago would have been probably a better time to share that little nugget of wisdom with Jacob. Jacob worked seven long years for Laban to have Rachel as his wife, and he ended up with Leah.

What a story! You may be thinking, "What a rip-off!" But, God, the King of all, knew everything and had everything under control. As this story unfolds you will see that everything really does work out for the best to those who love and serve the Lord.

GOD ALLOWED THE DECEIT

Imagine with me for a moment how Leah must have felt that night going to Jacob's tent. She was betraying her sister and her sisters fiancée. How did she feel in the morning when Jacob saw who she was and freaked out? I think about these things when I read the Bible. These were real people.

Leah probably felt like the chocolate-covered strawberry nougat wanting to be a chocolate-covered caramel. She must have been humiliated knowing that Jacob really did not want her to be his wife. It was clear he wanted and loved her beautiful little sister, Rachel. Leah knew she was not beautiful on the outside, compared to her sister. Then, to top it off, her very own father had to lie in order to get her married. Ever feel like a chocolate-covered strawberry nougat?

God allowed Laban to deceive Jacob so that Leah would be married. Is this hard to believe? This does not mean our holy God overlooks sin. What it means is that He works all things out for good to those that love and serve Him according to His perfect will. Laban's evil intent was worked out for Jacob's good, as well as Rachel's. In the end of the story, Laban's sin eventually brought him consequences that hurt his life. He lost his two girls and a great son-in-law, the best of his herds, and respect from his family. The sin infected his life. However, Leah's life and destiny went forward.

It is very apparent that God did not see Leah as others saw her. He saw a beautiful *Princess* being placed into her destiny. Our looks have nothing to do with being a *Princess*, daughter of the King. Remember that our physical looks are just as unique as the destinies that have been created for us. God had a *Princess* destiny for Leah, just as much as He had a *Princess* destiny for Rachel.

Leah's *Princess* plans were made before she was formed in her mother's womb. (See Psalm 139:16, nkjv.) Leah means "weary and uncertain." This was true in man's eyes, but not with God. He took her weariness and uncertainty and turned it for the good. God was positioning her so she could fulfill the destiny in which He created her to walk. Isn't that awesome! He used the deceit of Laban to work all things together for the good in Leah's life. She was made a chocolate-covered strawberry nougat for a reason.

It is such a comfort to know that the King knows exactly where to put us, when to do it, and how to fulfill it. God opens doors that no man can shut, and He shuts doors that no man can open. (See Revelation 3:7.) In Leah's case, we can say He opens and shuts tent flaps! He alone is the King and directs our lives. God's Kingdom is so different than the kingdom of this world. As His daughters we never have to be anxious or uneasy about our lives.

HE OPENS DOORS NO MAN CAN SHUT

On a ministry trip to Nigeria, Africa, I learned this lesson of trusting God to open doors, and I watched in amazement as He placed me where He needed me to be. I was with four other ladies ministering at a *Women of God International Conference* in Jos, Nigeria. The Governor and his wife in Jos were followers of Christ. His wife heard we were in the city, ministering to women. She came to one of the meetings and graciously extended an invitation for us to come to the mansion for a private luncheon.

This was exciting. It is not every day you get to have lunch at the governor's mansion! In Nigeria the governors are treated like royalty. The day came for our special luncheon. We all were excited. On the way there we were briefed on protocol. Protocol is extremely important; it is the "what to do and what not to do" list of manners. I listened intently, hoping to learn a thing or two before I formally met "Her Excellency."

At the Governor's Mansion

The mansion was beautiful and fully guarded, just like you would think a governors mansion would be. We were ushered into a private room of red velvet and French décor. Her Excellency greeted each of us individually before we sat down. As my hand touched hers, I saw an open vision of a field of golden wheat. I almost forgot my instructions of greeting her by this divine interruption. I tucked the vision away, smiled, and introduced myself. I was told where to sit and pondered what I had just seen. I thought, What an odd way to meet someone, Lord!

After introductions and photos were exchanged, there was some plain ol' "girl talk." Some of the nervous butterflies that were previously having a hay day in my stomach seemed to settle down to a flutter. It was easy to see the inner and outer beauty of Her Excellency.

One of her aides announced lunch was served, and we moved from the red velvet room. We found ourselves standing before the dining room door that was arrayed in a gorgeous swag of material. It was pulled back, and one by one our names were announced. We were then escorted to our special seats at the table. Once seated, we were all introduced to the other twenty-some guests that were invited. The majority of us in that dining room were women. All were followers of Christ, and represented a wide variety of Nigerians that held various ministry positions in the workplace and government. Also among the guests were a Nigerian TV camera crew and several journalists from the newspaper. Many cameras and lights filled the room for the event. We had no idea that this was going to be televised. We were definitely a box of mixed chocolates in that royal dining room!

SING, SISTER, SING

Being the music minister of our group, Her Excellency asked if I would sing a couple of songs after lunch. I smiled, took a deep breath, and politely responded with "Yes, it would be my pleasure." At this point I was ignoring the big knot tightening in my stomach. Ever get those?

I requested a microphone and CD player sound system. However, I had been in this situation many times before, and thankfully the Father has prepared me to sing with nothing if need be. I have learned from experience that when the King places me somewhere strategic that I best allow Him to use my vessel in any way He chooses. Whether or not I had music and a microphone, I was willing to sing. He always has a plan and a purpose to fulfill. Besides, when I am weak, He is strong. This will be the same for you, *Princess*!

Before lunch was served, Her Excellency spoke to the TV camera and addressed the television public as to what the luncheon was about. The leader of our group, Dawn Lundgren, sat directly to the right of Her Excellency. This was the seat reserved for the honored guest. Dawn's name means "Awakening, or the day breaker." That's Dawn! She delivered a ray of light for Nigeria as she gave a short message to the group at hand and to the television audience. Valencia (Her Excellency's name) also gave a strong and brief message of hope to her people. Valencia's name means "Strong." Both names fit these women to the tee.

THE KING HAD A PLAN

God was using this luncheon for a larger audience than what was in that formal dining room! Right after lunch

I was asked to sing. The King had a plan. He brought me to Africa for many purposes, and this was one of the many. Thankfully, a sound system was put together at the last possible moment, and I was able to sing with my CD tracks. His Holy Presence filled the room as we worshipped together in song. He unified that box of mixed chocolates in a second. It was precious and something I will never forget. What a privilege to serve the King.

This luncheon was televised in Nigeria and we heard later that a clip of it was even sent to CNN. When I returned home after that trip, I was informed that my music was being used for TV ads and fill-ins for Nigerian television. Our God and Father is awesome!

We were given beautiful gifts, and made many new friends that day. After the meeting, we said our good-byes and were quickly whisked off to our vehicle. About five minutes into the trip home I told Dawn the vision I saw as I met Valencia. Dawn said, "You saw the harvest of souls that is about to come into the country of Nigeria. Was the wheat golden brown?" I said, "Yes, it was all light brown." She said, "Now is the time to harvest souls." Just then I realized I had left my purse at the mansion in the dining room next to the sound system! My passport, money, and favorite lipstick were in it. Everything necessary for me to finish the ministry trip and get home was in there. Immediately Timothy Olanade, our dear ministry friend and host in Nigeria, turned the vehicle around and headed back to the mansion.

Valencia was still outside with some of her friends when we pulled up. I teased her that I just could not stay away and needed another hug. She smiled and had an aide escort me to locate my purse. Somehow I knew I would return to Nigeria again after that little ordeal. Seeing the visions of wheat fields, and then leaving my passport in the governor's mansion, seemed to say it loud and clear to me, "You will be back."

To my great delight, a few months after we were home, European evangelist Reinhardt Bonnke conducted the world's largest evangelistic outreach ever in Nigeria. Over three million people attended the event. The following December a church in Nigeria had over six million people attend their 'Congress' meeting. Can you believe it? These were just two of the many examples of "the fields in Nigeria being ready for harvest!"

The King opens doors that no man can shut. He places us where He wants us to be, and then brings us back if He so chooses. We do not need to worry or be anxious about our lives because He has already made a plan. We simply need to be obedient and yield to Him so that plan can unfold. We are prepackaged from birth. Everything from our looks to gifts and talents are all wrapped up and packaged for delivery!

WHAT ABOUT RACHEL?

Did Rachel ever marry Jacob? Why would our loving God allow something so crummy to happen to poor Rachel? From our perspective it seems awful. Maybe it was not as devastating as it seems. When Jacob went to Laban and protested about being given Leah rather than Rachel, Laban came up with a plan. (May I suggest that he had this plan seven years prior, but was just now letting Jacob in on the secret?) I told you earlier that it was not unusual for men to have many wives at this point in history. Laban told Jacob to finish out the week of wedding festivities for Leah, and at the end of the seven days he could also have Rachel as his wife. Then Laban made Jacob promise to work for another seven years to seal this contract. Because of Jacobs's love for Rachel, he agreed.

One week after Jacob was married to Leah he was given Rachel as his wife. Then Jacob was bound to his commitment of seven more years of work. Rachel was not forgotten. Rachel's name means: little lamb. God took care of this little lamb. Leah was not forgotten. God made certain of that also. You will not be forgotten either.

KINGDOM PURPOSES ARE AT STAKE

At the time, these two sisters did not know the destiny that they had in God's Kingdom—but God did! He had a plan. The twelve tribes of Israel came from these two women. Leah bore Jacob seven sons, Rachel had two, and the other three tribes came from their maidservants. You will have to read the rest of the story to figure that one out. They had quite the baby ordeal! Leah was able to have children and Rachel was barren for many years. Read for yourself in Genesis chapter 30 why Rachel was barren. This too was the hand of God.

It all was history in the making, or if you like, "His story" in the making. The King deposited in these sisters His plan for their lives before they were born, and then once born, positioned them, opened the doors, and it came to pass. He will do this for you, as well. How exciting to walk in the plans made just for you.

YOU ARE FEARFULLY AND WONDERFULLY MADE

When Leah married Jacob, she was his *Princess* forever. Although she was not Jacobs's first pick for a wife, God placed her there and no one could take that title away. She was "on the dock" and walking as Jacob's *Princess* because God called her to that place. Leah was just as fearfully and wonderfully made by the hand of God as Rachel. God had a plan and purpose for Leah's life as much as He did for Rachel's. The same is true for you and me.

You are called by name and crowned from the King of Kings. You were knitted together in your mother's womb, and fearfully and wonderfully made by the hand of God. Psalm 139:13–14 says, "For You formed my inward parts; You covered me in my mother's womb. I will praise You, for I am fearfully and wonderfully made." The Father, Son, and Holy Spirit were all involved and present when you were being formed. They know every detail of your life and destiny!

Therefore, whether you see yourself as a Leah or a Rachel, does not matter. Whether you think of yourself as a chocolate-covered strawberry nougat or a chocolate covered caramel matters not! The King sees you, He created you, and He says you are wonderfully made. He looks at our heart. As we walk out our destiny He is continually forming the character of Jesus in us. The King is actually more interested in our character development than our destiny. Without character development our destiny is tainted.

CHOCOLATE-COVERED CHARACTER

All of us are still learning how to be a *Princess* in His Kingdom. Our development and destiny go hand in hand. As we walk out our destiny and wait on the King, we get our character developed on the journey. Rachel was learning patience and long suffering with her ordeal of marriage and years of barrenness. He was chipping away all pride and bitterness from her life. Leah was being taught humility and mercy with her situations. I'm sure there were many more things God was working in their lives. Those were just the obvious character developments.

Remember that your title as *Princess* was given to you

because of Jesus. The Prince of Peace paid a high price for the crown you wear. His sacrificed life was the ultimate payment. It was freely given to you, but cost Him His life. It was priceless, and should not be taken lightly. Wear your crown in confidence of His dying love for you. You are special.

Character development helps protect the title of daughter of the Most High God. It is like the chocolate covering over the strawberry nougat. The nougat needs the covering, or it would squirt all over the box. One way you protect your Father's kingdom is by living a blameless life—not presenting an opportunity for others to point a finger of blame at you or find fault. Character development helps you learn to handle yourself as a mature daughter of God. When you blow it, handle it in grace and forgiveness; truly the way a daughter of the King would act. You now represent His kingdom in everything you say and do. Especially everything you do. It is true that actions speak louder than words.

YOU ARE NOT OF THIS WORLD— YOU ARE HIS PRINCESS

As a daughter of the King, you need to understand that you are not of this world. Yes, you live here now, but this is not your home. Eternity is your home and your final resting place. Never let this world dictate what you should look like or what you should do with your life. You belong to His Eternal kingdom, and walk by His ways, and carry out His will for your life. You are His *Princess* in His kingdom.

If this is hard for you to grasp, stop right now and ask the King to reveal to you the royalty you have in Him. Just say, "Father help! I need to know the royalty I have in You. Please reveal it to me." Do not let another day go by, walking down the dock as an imposter of your identity. He made you exactly the way you are for His glory; just like He did Leah and Rachel.

A REVELATION OF ROYALTY

One day I cried out to the Father to reveal my royalty in Him. He then revealed a simple thing to me in an intuitive vision. (When I say "intuitive vision," it is like seeing something in your mind. For example: when somebody says, "Picture an ice cream sundae with bananas and strawberries on top." In your mind's eye, you picture that sundae. That is what I mean by "intuitive vision.")

In this vision, I was standing before the Father. He was seated on His throne in a large ballroom. I could not actually see His face, but I knew it was Him. I was in a beautiful, long, white gown, and on my head I saw a crown. I somehow could feel the extreme love He had for me. It almost felt like a warm heat being poured over my head.

This simple revelation of His love for me has forever impacted my walk with Him as His royal daughter. I knew that He created me, loved me, accepted me; and I had a destiny in the Kingdom to fulfill. I somehow knew I no longer needed to push, shove, or manipulate my way to the top of anything in this world. I wore the crown of royalty that was a symbol of my destiny. My heart was so filled with His Fatherly love I could hardly stand it. It was not long after this revelation that I received the mandate to write this book. I have not been the same since.

I try and imagine that crown on my head often so I will remember what I am in Him. While shopping one day, I bought a little crown that looked like the one I saw in my mind. Sometimes I even wear it when I preach! I call myself *Princess* from time to time. My husband and kids even started calling me *Princess*! In my morning journaling to the Father, I use *Princess* as my code name.

Another day I was in a store shopping and I bought a sticker that said "*Princess.*" I stuck it on the bumper of my minivan. Am I going overboard? Who cares? The King loves me, and this revelation of being His *Princess* makes me want to tell the world. Seeing that I am His much-loved *Princess* has changed my life. I am learning to rest in this royalty He has given me.

KINGDOM PRINCESS VERSUS WORLDLY PRINCESS

We do not need to measure up to the world's idea of what a *Princess* should look like. Isn't that a relief? Some days you may not feel like a *Princess*, but it does not matter; you still are. Remember your walk in Him is a walk of faith. Faith believes in things your natural eyes cannot see. Believing what God's Word says is faith.

STAY ON THE DOCK AND WALK YOUR WALK

Rachel and Leah both had enough reasons throughout their lives to jump off the dock of their destiny. I am sure they both could have given up more than once. However, they did not, and we can learn from this. They continued to press forward despite the circumstances around them. If they had given up it would have changed the course of history. The twelve tribes of Israel are the roots of our Christianity. Jesus came from this lineage. They had a big role to play. What role do you have to play in history? You really will not know whose lives are touched by your existence until you are in eternity. Be a history maker for God.

That is why I encourage you to do whatever it takes to see and know that you are His *Princess*. See yourself as His

Princess; listen to the Father as He speaks to you. Understand and see your place in this royal family of God. Make a mark for His Kingdom. Walk down your tailor made dock of destiny knowing you were fearfully and wonderfully made for the King's good pleasure. Make your mark in His story as His daughter just like Rachel and Leah.

PERSONAL PRINCESS REFLECTIONS

1. List the character traits in your life that tells others you are His *Princess.*

2. List what you think others see in you that make them think you are His *Princess.*

3. Left alone we cannot make ourselves *Princesses.* We need the Father/King to make us His daughters. Have you tried to become a *Princess* on your own?

4. Could you do it? Why or why not?

5. What things did you try to do?

6. Think about a girl that is the total opposite of you, maybe even one that really bothers you. Can you see the *Princess* in her? Are you okay with her being a *Princess,* too? Be honest.

7. How do you handle jealousy?

8. Have you ever pushed someone off her dock?

9. Do you think that trying to see the *Princess* in others would help you treat each other differently? Why?

10. Do you think *Princesses* should stick together and stand up for one another? Why?

11. What are some circumstances that can potentially cause you to jump off the dock of your destiny?

12. How did this chapter affect you personally?

Chapter 5

TAMAR: THE TAINTED PRINCESS

THE LIKELIHOOD OF being hurt physically, emotionally, or spiritually since your royal crowning as *Princess* is great. On a daily basis, many situations arise that make it easy for us to create an offense towards others in our hearts. Just think how something as small as a wrong look from a friend has the potential to affect us, not to mention the many situations that happen each day in our imperfect world. With all this opportunity for hurt to happen, you need to know that taking up an offense will taint (or discolor) your relationship with the Prince of Peace and the King of eternity.

Let's look at how to deal properly with hurts and wounds as a *Princess* of the King. You will find that even our own brothers and sisters in this kingdom will hurt us knowingly and unknowingly from time to time. That is why we must learn how to deal with this issue properly.

I found a *Princess* in the Bible that stunted her future by not dealing properly with her hurts and wounds. Her name was Tamar. She is not a role model in the positive sense. However, you can learn from her mistakes. She was one of King David's daughters, and therefore, a *Princess* in King David's Kingdom. You can read the story in 2 Samuel 13:1–33. Tamar lived in a different culture, with no rights. Today, women have a voice and can speak up when it comes to abusive situations. In any case of abuse in today's society, it is not a virtue to remain silent. You need to go to the proper authorities in your life for help. Parents, teachers, family, and social workers are there for you in any case of abuse. In Tamar's day, there was no such support system available.

Amnon Targets Tamar

King David had many wives, so Tamar had many half-brothers and half-sisters. Amnon was one of Tamar's half-brothers. Amnon always looked at Tamar with ungodly lust in his eyes and heart. The laws of the land, in this area of Israel, forbid any marriage or sexual relations with whole or half brothers or sisters. As a son of King David, Amnon knew well this law of the land. However, the law of the land was not enough to stop him from thinking lustful thoughts about Tamar. He actually started believing his own lie—that he could have Tamar as his own and began plotting how to capture her. Amnon's thoughts eventually turned into actions.

The virgin daughters of the King were kept in a protected area away from all men; even those that were close relatives (such as brothers). No men were permitted to see them without the presence of witnesses, which was a type of bodyguard in those days. Therefore, Amnon had no way of telling Tamar of his affections for her. How to contact her became the problem over which he was brooding; so much so that he became vexed and fell sick for his sister. Amnon was obviously mentally, spiritually, and physically deranged.

His state of mind was beginning to be obvious to those around him. Amnon's cousin Jonadab saw him one day and asked Amnon why he was always unhappy. Amnon told him, "I love Tamar, my brother Absalom's sister." So Jonadab slyly said to Amnon, "Go to bed and pretend you are sick; and when your father David comes to see you, say to him let my sister Tamar come and give me food. Prepare it in my sight..." (2 Sam. 13:4–5, AMP).

With that advice, Amnon did exactly that. He went home, pretended to be sick, and soon the King came to see him. Amnon said to the King, "Please let Tamar my sister come and make a couple of cakes for me in my sight that I may eat from her hand" (2 Sam. 13:6, nkjv). So King David believed Amnon was ill and sent for Tamar to prepare food and feed Amnon.

TAMAR WAS SET UP

When Tamar got to Amnon's house, she began to knead the dough for the cakes. When the cakes were done baking, she tried to give them to Amnon, but he refused to eat. He then ordered all of the men witnesses to leave the house. After they were gone he grabbed hold of Tamar. In 2 Samuel 13:12 Ammon says, "...Come my sister and lie with me." In verses twelve and thirteen, she responded, "No, my brother, do not force me, for no such thing should be done in Israel. Do not do this disgraceful thing! And I, where could I take my shame? And as for you, you would be like one of the fools of Israel. Now therefore, please speak to the king; for he will not withhold me from you." In verse fourteen it states that Ammon would not heed her voice; and being stronger than she, he forced her and lay with her. (See 2 Samuel 13:12–14, NKJV.) At that point Tamar was not responsible for the wrong choice Ammon made.

When Amnon's sinful act was over, hatred rose in him towards Tamar. She now represented to him his very black sin. He hated her more now than he ever thought he had loved her. Looking at her, he commanded her to leave his house. She said to him, "Sending me away is even worse than the other that you did to me!" (2 Sam. 13:16, knjv). But he would not listen to her and called his servant to throw her out of his house and had the doors bolted behind her.

She was treated like a prostitute. No words could ever adequately express Tamar's feelings of betrayal and fear that now plagued her body, mind, and soul. This was a clear case of rape, which took away her virginity. In Tamar's culture, the virginity of women was sacred and highly honored. She knew no man in this society would want to marry a tainted *Princess.*

The Violated Princess

All the virgin daughters of King David wore beautiful colored robes to signify their royalty and inheritance. Tamar had been clothed in one of these virgin gowns. When Amnon violated her title as a virgin *Princess* of King David, she could not bear to wear the royal gown. In her eyes she was now a tainted (stained) *Princess.* Tamar fell to the ground in despair and threw ashes on her head as she tore apart her royal robe. She then held her hand up to her face and wept out loud. She was deeply wounded by this ungodly, selfish act of Amnon.

In her sadness, she turned to her full-blooded brother, Absalom. In those days, full-blooded brothers were like a guardian to their full-blooded sisters. King David had so many children that it was almost as though Absalom played the role of father to Tamar. Therefore, it was natural for her to go to Absalom in her despair. When Absalom saw her coming, he knew Tamar was carrying bad news. Without one word yet spoken from her mouth, Absalom could tell what had happened by the look upon her face, the ashes upon her head, and the torn royal robe.

Tamar told Absalom the whole story of what Amnon did to her. Absalom, not wanting King David to find out about this tragedy, told her not to tell anyone and had her move into his home. He was very angry with Amnon and wanted to kill him for hurting Tamar. He knew that the humiliation of being raped now affected the rest of her life. Her chances of marriage and children were low, because no man would marry a tainted *Princess.* Therefore, Tamar hid in shame at Absalom's house. In 2 Samuel 13:20 (amp), it says, "The rest of Tamar's life was lived as a desolate (alone, forsaken, lonely, stripped, and devastated) woman" (author's paraphrase.) How tragic is that?

This seems like a harsh story to read from the Bible, doesn't it? Sometimes it is hard to believe these things really took place. Nevertheless, they did, and they still do take place in our time! There is nothing new under the sun. (See Ecclesiastes 1:9, NKJV.) Evil has been here as long as Adam and Eve. However, as I stated before, women have a voice in today's society to speak out in the case of rape. Even in the case of emotional and verbal abuse, there is help for you to seek out. Thank God!

WHAT CAN WE LEARN FROM THIS TRAGEDY?

So what can we learn from this story? First we can learn from Amnon's sin. He had ungodly thoughts about Tamar that possessed him. Obviously Amnon had a root of lust that needed to be dealt with. His continuous lust for Tamar was deeply embedded in him. For Amnon to try and change his way of thinking by relying on his own strength probably would not have worked. That was why his ungodly thoughts eventually led to sin.

If you do not allow the Lord to change your thinking, you are subject to ungodly thoughts. You will reap what you have sown in your thought life. As a daughter of the King, you are instructed to take every thought captive unto the obedience of Jesus Christ. How do you do that? It's easy. When a thought comes your way that you know is ungodly and evil, do not deny it; acknowledge it and say, "I take that thought captive unto the obedience of Jesus Christ." Christ is the head of the body and any thoughts you have must submit to the head. Sometimes you just need to remind your mind!

Remember, if you are caught in a thought cycle that bombards you and you try to change, but find yourself thinking the same thoughts, you will need to ask the Lord to reveal why. We covered this topic in the Cinderella Chapter.

You may be saying, "But I have never thought like Amnon; he was really bad." Yes, what he did was bad, but sin is sin. The only thing that differs with sin is the consequence you pay for that sin once it is birthed.

If you are having a hard time relating Amnon and Tamar's story to your own life, let me make it simpler for you.

A Clique and a Deadly Letter

This story of jealousy happened to a girl in my class when I was in eighth grade. One of the leaders of our "cool group" had a fight with a certain girl in the "not so cool group." So our fearless leader devised a plan of action against this girl, and we all went along with it. Not going along with it was taking a chance of being kicked out of the cool group. Have you been in that situation? Here a clique, there a clique, everywhere a clique clique. You will find cliques in every group of people upon the earth. As a *Princess* you must learn how to avoid these cliques and love everyone. Cool group or not.

Well, to "set her straight" we all wrote her a letter and signed it, telling her how much we hated her. I will never forget what it did to that girl. It was so hurtful to her. Later, I was ashamed I took part in the letter. I was part of a lie-planting scheme of the devil.

This was an elementary example, but it makes a point. Sharing evil thoughts with others can birth sin, just like our leader did with us. Amnon shared his evil thoughts in the same manner about Tamar with his friend Jonadab. Amnon's sin was birthed right then. Let's take it a step farther.

When we all agreed together about our mutual friend's problem, we gave birth to that thought of jealousy. Once it was birthed, we needed to feed the ugly little demon named jealousy. Thus, we devised the insidious plan to write this girl a letter that told her how we all really felt about her.

We began justifying why she needed to know these things. We fed jealousy when we wrote the letter. The letter was then signed, sealed, and delivered. When she received this letter, she was still under the impression that we were her friends. When she read the letter she was hurt; and when she saw who it was from she was crushed. What we did planted a lie into a precious soul that God the Father loves, and sent His only Son to die for. Sin gave birth to death.

Amnon planted a lie into Tamar after he raped her. Tamar was under the impression that she was safe to bake cakes because Amnon was her half brother. He was family. When he violated her, she was crushed. Get the picture? He threw her out of his house and cast her aside like a nobody. Immediately she bought the lie and believed she was a nobody. It was planted in her through his sin and brought forth death to a *Princess.*

Sin Only Comes in One Size— Big and Ugly

Every bad thought will eventually lead to sin if you do not take each one captive unto the obedience of Christ. Sin is sin; only the consequences differ. In the law of our land, murder or rape is obviously going to create deeper consequences in your life than a nasty letter to a friend. Nevertheless, in God's eyes, sin is sin. We raped not only this girl's heart, but also her soul. We abused that girl's heart and soul, and it is painful for me to think that I hurt a person God so loves.

You can fall prey to this sin of jealousy and slander at any age. You can abuse someone emotionally and spiritually by your jealousy and slander, using the telephone or e-mail. The second an ungodly thought is spoken or acted out, it is birthed. Did you know that thinking wrong thoughts and letting them go wild in your mind is like actually doing it in God's eyes? The Father can and does read our hearts and e-mails. (See 1 Samuel 16:7.)

Whatever You Sow, You Will Reap Its Harvest

"For whatever you sow [your thoughts, attitudes, actions], that he will also reap" (Gal. 6:7, NKJV, author's paraphrase). It is just like planting corn. If you put a seed of corn into the ground, you would expect a corn plant to grow. If you sow (plant) envy and jealousy, you will eventually reap envy and jealousy. If you sow a mean letter, you will reap a mean letter. That same type of mean letter has come around in my mailbox. I participated in sowing hate and pain through that letter, and I reaped hatred and pain from others who wrote to me years later when they had issues with me. This is *not* what a *Princess* is meant to reap.

This law also works for the good. If you sow money into God's kingdom, you will reap God's blessing on your finances. If you sow generously, you will reap generously. If you sow kindness, you will reap kindness. I have given away coats, clothes, and money. Be a sower of righteousness, peace, and joy. This is what a *Princess* like you is meant to reap!

SIN SEPARATES US FROM THE FATHER

As we continue to look at the story of Tamar you will see the consequences to rape are different than the consequences to slander or gossip, but both of these sins will equally separate us from the King. Sin always has and always will separate us from the Father.

After Amnon raped Tamar, he could no longer look at King David, his father, in the face. His heart was separated from his father through his sin. He was a prisoner to that sin. He sowed death to a *Princess*. He would eventually reap death himself if he did not repent. The same principle is true for us as daughters of the King. We, too, cannot look our Father in the face when we have sin in our lives. We, too, are prisoners of that sin until we repent. Without repentance we will reap eternal death.

Daily, I ask for forgiveness and protection from wrong thoughts. I pray, "Lord, cleanse my thoughts and let the words of my mouth and meditation of my heart be acceptable in Your sight." I paraphrased Psalm 19:14 to be a prayer. Changing your way of thinking to His way of thinking brings life!

Remember when Absalom made the vow to kill Amnon?

Well, two years later he did. Here is another example from this story of a bad thought that eventually came to pass. Absalom plotted out Amnon's death, and those non-captive bad thoughts gave birth to sin. The sin was murder.

The First Lesson: We Must Take Every Thought Captive

The first lesson learned from this story is to take every thought captive. We are not to entertain ungodly thoughts, or let them past our mouth. As *Princesses,* we need a pure heart and mind. Take those thoughts captive and do not give them one single breath of life from your mouth. The words you speak take on life, because the creator lives in you. (See 2 Corinthians 10:5.) Make sure they are words of life and not death. He changes our way of thinking when we meditate on His word, His beauty, and His love. You will begin to only let life come out of your mouth.

If a bad thought or wicked thought patterns continually bombard your mind, and you find yourself battling it daily, you may need to take a stronger action against it. Go back to the Cinderella chapter to help you deal with it properly.

The Second Lesson: We Can Be Free Through Forgiveness

The second lesson we can learn from this story is from Tamar. It is our Father's desire that His *Princesses* are free to walk the dock without any baggage. Tamar was not a free *Princess* after this abuse happened to her. She did not deal with this hurt and wound properly and carried this baggage until she died. She had a sad ending to her story. She lived as a desolate woman the rest of her life because she held an offense against Amnon. Desolate means: alone, forsaken, lonely, stripped, and devastated.

Her title of *Princess* could not be taken away from her, but she could not see that. She chose to hide in shame and unforgivness until she was an old woman. Although Amnon raped her, the truth was that she remained a *Princess*. She believed the lie planted in her that she was now a nobody. How sad.

The wounds and pain of the abuse blinded her from seeing the *Princess* she still was. She was born into King David's household and no one could take that title from her. She allowed that evil spirit in Amnon to take away her title as *Princess*. Do not allow any demonic spirit to steal, kill, or destroy your title as *Princess*. John 10:10 says, "The thief does not come except to steal, and to kill, and to destroy. I have come that they (*Princesses*) may have life, and that they may have it more abundantly." Take the abundant life He freely gives you, *Princess*, it is the royal way. The battle is in the mind so cast those ungodly thoughts out! Watch for those that would be used of the enemy to plant lies in you.

Like Tamar, you and I have beautiful colored robes that represent our royalty as daughters of the King. Our robes get ripped and torn from time to time just because we live in this sinful world. We do not have to wear ripped robes, but they will remain ripped if we do not forgive and let go of things that wound and hurt us in our daily walk on the dock. Jesus is our Restorer and He restores our robes to perfection when we let go and forgive. Isn't that comforting to know?

THE OLD BAGGAGE MUST BE DUMPED

Sometimes it is very hard to forgive a sin that has been done to you, especially if you were deeply wounded. Some of the worst wounds and hurts can come from others in the kingdom of God, just like Tamar's greatest wound was from a member of her father's own kingdom. If we carry around that baggage, we too could end up like Tamar. She could not see herself as a *Princess* daughter of the King any longer, and she eventually was a lonely, desolate, and devastated old woman.

As *Princesses* we must forgive continually. As we forgive, the lies will not be able to attach themselves to us in any way. We must love like our lives depend on it (and it does). We must walk in grace. If you need to forgive someone, don't let time elapse on that situation. It will only cause you more pain. His light needs to shine on that darkness immediately.

Forgiveness is a powerful weapon in the kingdom of God. It would have released Tamar from being a desolate old woman, but she chose to let the offense stay. Forgiveness will release us, too. Forgiveness opens the door so His light can shine in, remove all evil, and heal our hearts. Once the hurt and pain is removed, He gives you more of His strength to continue to walk the dock as a *Princess.*

The Third Lesson: Do Not Hide in Darkness; Come Into the Light

While on a ministry trip with Dawn Lundgren, I was in the southern island region of the Philippines. This region has a steamy tropical climate. Since there were no hotels in this area, we stayed at the home of the local pastor and his wife who hosted the women's conference. These tropical homes are very basic. Most have no running water, which means no flushing toilets, sink water, shower, or bathtubs.

We were blessed to have in this particular home, in the basement, a bathroom with a flushing toilet, and a sink with running water. My friend Audra and I were so thankful. This little luxury was like having a piece of heaven on earth. However, there was one "thing" that stood in the way of using that basement bathroom. That "thing" was the twelve-inch very much alive green lizard lurking on the basement steps' wall. Yes, I said twelve-inch lizard! This creature was not their pet, but it was allowed to live in their home for the sole purpose of eating other rodents and harmful bugs.

Actually, there were many small lizards hanging on the walls and ceilings. The smaller ones became almost invisible to me as the week progressed. However, the big ones were a different story! I don't know if I would have ever gotten used to them. But, God gave me the grace for that week to handle it just fine. Thank you, Father!

In this particular home we used flashlights in the middle of the night if we had to use the basement bathroom. The flashlight lit our way down the stairs and past the enormous lizard's hangout. The light would pierce the darkness on the cement floor, causing a frantic explosion of scurrying bugs. The roaches and other nocturnal bugs would dive for cover under boards on the floor and into wall cracks.

Creepy things thrive in the darkness. They are more comfortable with dark than they are in light. That is why they scatter for the darkness again. Escaping from the intrusion of light was their only mission at this point. My mission was going to the bathroom and getting upstairs as quickly as possible.

WOUNDS LIKE TO HIDE IN DARKNESS

Wounds and hurts we take on are just like those creepy things in the night. They try to scatter away from any light shining on them when they are exposed. If we allow them to stay and hide, they will. Tamar's unforgiveness caused her to remain a prisoner. She allowed that creepy thing to stay. When you find yourself making excuses for your behavior, you have already stepped over that line of allowing creepy things to stay. Amnon wounded Tamar deeply; so that unhealed wound was an open door for a spirit of control to come in. Instead of being healed and living a happy life the spirit of control had its ugly way.

Avoiding the Control Spirit

When we do not give up these wounds or grudges against others, we open ourselves up to a spirit of control. A spirit of control was working through Absalom, and it targeted Tamar. You might be saying, "But Robin, Absalom did not hurt Tamar. He helped her and cared for her." Yes, Absalom did take her into his home being that she was his full-blooded sister. However, remember he made her hide and not tell her father King David of the rape.

Hiding from her father only added fuel to the fire of hatred she had towards Amnon. Now she not only was a tainted *Princess,* but also kept a dark secret from her father, King David. Absalom hindered her from receiving her father's love and comfort by telling her to keep this a secret. He took matters into his own hands, rather than going to the King. Anyone that does not point you to the Father when you have been hurt is not doing what is right. That is control and manipulation.

We do not need to hide from our Father. We can tell Him anything! Absalom was wrong to hide Tamar. His influence caused her to live a desolate life. That same spirit of control is still alive today. It lurks around, looking for wounded, hurt people. If you open yourself up to its evil influence, it will make you think it is taking care of you.

It will influence you to put up walls, and keep you feeling bitter toward the person or persons that have hurt you. Its mission is to keep you angry, so you remain bitter. Bitterness eats away at the core of our inner man and robs us of our full fellowship with the Father. Eventually, it will teach you to never trust others. The sad fact of the matter is that this control spirit must use a human vessel to work. So beware! If anyone or anything ever keeps you or is keeping you from coming into the light and forgiving others, run from it. Your destiny is at stake.

BACK TO FORGIVENESS ONCE AGAIN

Forgiveness is what will keep that spirit of control away. You have been forgiven, and so you are commanded to forgive those that hurt you. If you do not forgive, your Father will not forgive you. Matthew 6:14 says, "For if you forgive men their trespasses, your heavenly Father will also forgive you. But if you do not forgive men their trespasses, neither will your Father forgive your trespasses." Trespasses are sins others commit against you. As the King's *Princess* you do not have to become desolate like Tamar from bending your knee to the spirit of control and manipulation. Hiding in shame is no way for a *Princess* to live. Forgive, and go on.

WE NEED TO WEAR "GRACE" LIPSTICK

Proverbs 22:11 says, "He who loves purity of heart and has grace on his lips, the King will be his friend." I love that verse! We are made pure when we become children of God through Jesus, but remember He is continually cleansing us of our sins. Each day we have many opportunities to sin. When necessary, we ask for and give out forgiveness. This process will continue throughout our lifetime. Once the sin is gone, your heart is again pure. When our hearts are pure, our mouths will speak purely in return. For out of the abundance (overflow) of the heart his mouth speaks. (See Luke 6:45.) Keep that grace lipstick on at all times! Forgiveness releases kindness and mercy into your life and into the lives of others. You are the righteousness of Christ!

Walk in Purity and Grace

When you walk in purity, His grace will naturally flow out from you. That grace is like a fresh spring of water flowing out of the ground that is cool and refreshing. Wounds, hurts, and lies will dam up that spring of life inside of you. Have you ever been around a pond that has no fresh water flowing in or out of it? It usually has a green murky layer on top and smells. If someone in the kingdom walks in unforgiveness, everyone they touch is slimed. Life does not flow in or out of them because of the dam of unforgiveness.

In the King's presence, you will experience times of His glorious light illuminating the sin in your heart. You may not have seen it until that very moment. It may be a sin He has been convicting you of for some time. He will gently reveal it during worship, a teaching, while meditating on His word, or even while visiting with a friend. Have no fear—let Him go after the slime on the pond! It could be anything like impure thoughts, prideful attitudes, selfishness, anger, or unforgiveness. Whatever the label, let Him take it away so you can walk freely with no baggage.

When we are walking in grace and forgiveness, we are as a refreshing spring of crystal clear water. Anyone that comes near us will be refreshed. The King pours life into us, and then we pour it out on others. Life goes in, and life comes out—rivers of living water flowing out of our inner most being. Our Father God, the King of the universe, is pleased when we let Him into our lives and then let Him be poured out through us.

BE A FRUITFUL ROYAL PALM TREE

A *Princess* of the Most High King handles hurts and wounds by forgiving and forgetting what lies behind. She presses forward to the high calling on her life. No *Princess* should live a desolate, tainted life like Tamar. Tamar's name means "Palm Tree." A palm is a flourishing, tall, and upright tree. Its branches are a symbol of victory. The royal palm is known to attract the eye wherever it is seen. Living in South Florida allows me to take in the palms' beauty every day.

We need to see this message of Tamar from every angle. Her name is symbolic. Tamar could have continued to flourish, be upright, and walk in victory had she gone to the Father in the first place. Her name was her destiny. It is interesting that a palm tree is known to attract the eye wherever it is seen. We as the Body of Christ should also attract the eyes of the world to reveal Christ to them. We are the branches waved in victory; preparing the way of the Lord. We are to walk in victory and uprightness.

TAKE CARE OF THE PALM

It is known that palm trees need good soil and proper care to be healthy and prosperous. The type of soil determines the quantity of nutrients and water the plant receives. The palm tree needs proper fertilization. Without this proper care, fungus will appear and cause "bud rot." Bud rot will occur in the heart of the fruit in the palm, and the tree will wilt and die. This is exactly what happened to Tamar. She allowed an infection to enter her, and it caused her destiny to wilt and die.

We, as children of God, can glean a lot of truth just from the proper care of the palm tree. Taking every thought captive is like maintaining proper soil in our hearts so God's word may grow ever deeper in us. You will fertilize this soil in your heart by forgiving others. By doing this you will grow strong, live victoriously, and not develop fungus rot. You are a beautiful, robed daughter of the King. Do not look back. Go ahead, move forward, and walk the dock with a pure heart using gracious words as you go. Never allow the past to stop the glorious future He has for you!

Personal Princess Reflections

1. Amnon sinned by raping Tamar, deeply affecting her life. Can you relate? Maybe you cannot relate to rape. How do you relate?
2. What does the Bible say we should do when someone deeply hurts us?
3. What happens when you forgive others?
4. As you read this chapter, did the Holy Spirit reveal anything in your life that you are hiding from the King's light?
5. How easy is it to keep those things hidden?
6. List all the different options Tamar had in her situation.
7. Next to that list of options, write down the results that would have taken place with each. What was the best option?
8. When you are hurt, do you look at your options and choose what is best?
9. Why is it easy to have our emotions choose our options?
10. In what way did this chapter touch your life?

Chapter 6

You Were Born for Such a Time As This

For a moment, think about all the lessons or activities you are involved in or have experienced in the past: dance class, photography, computer programming, debate club, writing, poetry, scouting, drawing, sports, languages, sewing, cooking, nursing, Bible studies, Sunday school, and so forth. God is using everything in your life to mold you into the image of His Son so that you will become all He created you to be in His kingdom. He uses the good things right alongside of the seemingly bad. Sometimes you have to get older before you see how it all fits together, but that is the fun of it.

Looking back, I see why I was in theatre, dance, speech, writing, and music. Natural talents and abilities flow alongside of His plans for our lives. I also see the painful experiences that have been used to create His plans and purposes to be fulfilled in me. Because I love and obey Him, He has taken the things meant for evil in my life and used them for the good. The Father knows every stage of your destiny. Remember He created you, wrote down all the days of your life in a book, and only you can fulfill that call. It is up to you to walk in His divine will; He did not make us robots. If you look closer at your life, and ask Him to reveal it to you, you will see His plan for your life.

Your Name Has a Special Meaning and Purpose

Your name speaks out your destiny. It is a full representation of who you are. Every time someone says your name your destiny is being proclaimed. For me they are saying, "Robin, you shine with fame." My name, *Robin,* means "shining with fame." My middle name, *Renee,* means "re-born." Throughout my life, I have found myself *shining with fame* on platforms of many sizes, in front of various crowds for various reasons. Talent contests, dramas, and singing were usually at least one of the reasons. Before I became a kingdom *Princess,* the main reason for my being on any platform boiled down to my own selfish interests and desire for fame.

However, once I was re-born into His kingdom, my reasons to be in front of people changed. It was no longer for me, but for Him. I wanted to tell others about this kingdom. It is a lie to say my old flesh does not try to emerge and steal His glory from time to time. This *Princess* thing is a process; we are ever learning to decrease so He might increase within us. He will use our natural abilities to bring glory to His Son Jesus.

The Father continually places me in front of people to shine forth his fame, and advance His kingdom. When I start shining for my own self-interest, He knows just what to do. He is a perfect agent, and has a perfect plan. Our destinies all unfold in His perfect time. We need not be anxious or worry about anything. He is never late.

We are usually the ones rushing to our destinations. He places us wherever we need to be whenever He says it is the right time.

Your name is also proclaiming your destiny every time it is spoken. Have you ever looked at your name and what it means? You may think your mother and father named you, but the Bible says He knew your name even before you were born. (See Isaiah 49:1.) If you do not know what your name means, look your name up in a book of names. Think about it. Your name, which reveals your destiny, has been called out over you ever since your birth! Every day your destiny is proclaimed. When anybody says your name, they are declaring what you are.

ESTHER, THE BITTERSWEET STAR

The story of Esther in the Bible is a great example of this. Esther's name means: "star, and myrtle or bittersweet." She was a star to her people. The starring role of queen was her destiny, and that role was bittersweet. She is an incredible example to us as a royal daughter of the Most High God. Many examples and teachings have come from this book, I will only be touching on a small portion of who Esther was and represented. If you ever get the chance to read other teachings in regards to this book, I encourage you to do so!

Reading the Book of Esther is worth every letter, comma, and period. For this chapter you will need to read the story for yourself, if you have never done so. Let me give you an overview, until you can read it for yourself.

BRIEF OVERVIEW OF THE STORY

The story begins with King Ahasuerus dumping the beautiful Queen Vashti because of her unwillingness to come to him when he called for her. She was dethroned and kicked out of the kingdom on the seventh day of the seventh week of the King Ahasuerus' party. Now she was no longer Queen Vashti, but just plain Vashti. The name Vashti means: "lovely, and thread." A thread is not strong. Once cut, it is irreparable. Once lovely Vashti was cut off, it was irreparable.

I have some advice: never ever say, "No" to the King of Kings when He calls you. There is safety in obedience, and He deserves our respect. Queen Vashti may have had many excuses to deny the King of her presence, but those excuses were obviously not good enough to turn down the King when he called for her. How much more do we need to heed the call of our King and Father when He is calling us to sit with Him, go somewhere, or do something? Enough said.

Now the king, although he made this harsh decision, was without a queen and became despondent. A sweeping search of young virgins was made in the land to find a new queen for the king. Sounds like the timeless story of Cinderella, doesn't it? Esther was one of the beauties collected within the region. Her uncle Mordecai knew in his heart that God was up to something when Esther left for the palace. He knew Esther was special. It was God's sovereign plan to have Mordecai, in that city, raising Esther "for such a time as this." (See Esther 4:14.) As with Esther, God, the King of the universe, knows exactly where you are, where to find you, and where to put you for fulfilling His divine destiny for your life. I wonder if this is where the saying, "You are fit for a king!" comes from.

Let the Spa Treatments Begin

Esther was taken to the palace and placed with all the other beautiful virgins. However, it took a year before any of the virgins could be considered proper enough to meet the King. They were kept in a section of the palace that was the yearlong preparation parlor—the ultimate day spa. Here, they were prepared inside and out to be fit for the King.

Off the bat, God gave Esther favor from the "keeper of the women." Esther received seven maids and was given the best suite in the palace during the yearlong wait to meet the king. It was nothing she or her Uncle Mordecai bought, did, or said to give her this favor. She did not scratch, bite, or claw her way to the top. God Almighty caused favor to come to her. Esther was a young woman of grace. Remember that grace makes you friends of kings.

MYRRH AND SPICE SPA TREATMENTS

So what did these girls do for a year? Certain purification steps were taken during that yearlong wait before you were presented to the King. As a mater of fact, daily beauty treatments were required. Can you imagine a year of beauty treatments day in and day out. Take me away! Over the first six months, Esther had daily massages with oil of myrrh. The second half of the year, perfume and spice oils were used. Thus, you have bitter and sweet.

Myrrh oil was expensive and very valuable in Bible times. This herb was pressed into oil that was then worked into their skin. It is considered a bitter herb. Remember what Esther's name means in Hebrew? This myrrh oil was used to detoxify (cleanse) their systems inside and out. Its medicinal purposes killed germs, healed wounds, and even helped alleviate pain. It was one of the oils given to Jesus by the three wise men. Hebrews used this oil to bury their dead.

The oil of spice and perfume helped soften the skin,

and gave it fragrance. This was a sweet fragrance. Both oils were a necessary part of Esther's preparation to meet the King; your *Princess* process requires the same of you. As a *Princess* you are being prepared to meet the King. You will go through these same beauty treatments, but in a different sort of way. You will experience both the bitter and sweet in life.

WE GET SPA TREATMENTS BY THE HOLY SPIRIT

How do you go through these same beauty treatments? You too will get a rub down with the oil of myrrh from time to time to remove toxins. However, I am not talking about the toxins that are in your natural body. I am referring to the toxins that make you unhealthy in your spirit. Toxins that affect your spirit come from sin. If sin is not removed, your spirit becomes unhealthy. The Father will then find it necessary to help detoxify you.

In your life you will actually go back and forth from the myrrh season to the sweet spice and perfume season. Although it may be a harder season to understand, the myrrh season needs to be fully embraced so you may become the *Princess* He desires you to be.

When the myrrh has been embraced, you will find the spice and perfume season following shortly thereafter. This season is always a special time. Everything in your life will have a sense of purpose and destiny. Your attitude and appreciation for life will be right on the mark. You will feel as though you could meet the King of Kings face to face at anytime. Your countenance is sweet towards others, and you are a sweet smelling fragrance to the Lord.

As you mature in kingdom life, you will find the myrrh seasons come less frequent and are shorter in length, while the perfume and spice seasons will grow to be longer and more frequent. His ultimate goal for you is to eventually be pure and spotless for His Son—a sweet smelling aroma for the Prince.

MOUNTAINTOP AND VALLEY EXPERIENCES

We go in and out of these seasons all through our lives until we are face to face with Him in eternity. Another name for this is "mountaintop and valley experiences" in our walk. Everyone goes through them; it is part of the plan. It would be great to be able to stay on the mountaintop of spice and perfume all of the time, but the valleys of myrrh help shape us. Without the valleys, we would not grow. Without the mountains, we would not have hope to go through the valleys.

TIME TO MEET THE KING

The Word tells us that King Ahasuerus was in his seventh year of ruling as King, when Esther was finished with the beauty treatments and officially presented before him. God's timing is perfect for all of our destinies. She was obviously worth the wait for King Ahasuerus. Out of all the beauties, Esther won his heart, favor, and the golden crown as the new queen.

The number seven in the Bible symbolizes "completion." The book of Esther is loaded with this number. Queen Vashti was dumped on the seventh day of the seventh week of the King's celebration. Esther had seven maids assigned to her during preparation time. Seven was the number of years of King Ahaurases' reign as King when Esther was crowned. She was the star player to complete God's plan for the Hebrew people in that time and the number seven signified that. You will see that all things in the Kingdom have meaning to God, even numbers.

Esther Was Full of Grace

Esther was a brave, beautiful, and graceful queen. In her fifth year reigning as queen, she was asked of God to do the incredible task of saving the Jewish people from complete extermination. By God's grace, she did what she was asked to do. The number *five* is the number of "grace." See how this works? The Bible is full of symbols. God's grace was on Esther because she was willing and obedient to His call. Remember grace on lips makes you friends to kings?

God put her where He needed her to be to do the job she was destined to do. She was born for such a time as this. She was created to look the way she did, live where she lived, and be placed in the palace at a very specific time. Remember, God is the one who opens doors that no one can shut and shuts doors that no one can open. (See Revelation 3:7.)

So many things in our lives have symbolic meaning. You just need to pay attention to details to see them.

The Number Seven—Completion

The number *seven* has special meaning in my life, too. When my husband Chuck and I had been married for four years we decided to have children, but never were able to conceive. We began to get upset about the whole deal. Our doctor ran many tests to see what the problem might be. The tests revealed that Chuck needed surgery. This was done, and we waited to see if now we would conceive.

We were both Spirit-filled believers and loved the Lord when we married. By far, this was the biggest test of faith I had come up against in my life. We waited and prayed. I would cry often. No different results came from having surgery. My dream of being a mommy was fading fast. I definitely would categorize this time in my life as a rub down with the oil of myrrh, a real valley.

I began blaming God for not answering my prayer. My faith was obviously very rocky at that time. My faith was not really in God, but in the doctors to create a miracle. I became angry and bitter towards God for not answering my prayer like I thought He should and when I thought He should. Every Mother's Day that went by, I would cry and become bitterer because I had no baby to call me "Mother."

I had the nerve to say to God, "If You are not going to give me children, then I am going to do something else with my life." It was like I was shaking my fist toward heaven when I said this. This is called rebellion towards God. Rebellion opens the door to many evil things. When there is strife and rebellion every sort of evil is present: jealousy, anger, immorality, rage, and the like. I opened that door.

SCHOOL WAS NOT THE ANSWER

I thought going back to school and having a career would ease the pain and help me run away from the whole ordeal. However, it only made matters worse. The very day I started school, our marriage began to suffer. I had opened the door to evil influence because of my open rebellion to God. God had a sovereign plan for my life, but I could not see it through the pain of not being able to have a baby. The demons of darkness were trying to make that sovereign plan all the more hard to see with each passing day.

Months went by, and I tried to fill the void of having no child with worldly things. However, being in rebellion towards my Father was causing me to feel empty inside.

The Running Was Over

Seven months went by when I finally came to the end of my bitterness towards my heavenly Father. You can only run away so long before the emptiness overtakes you. Thank God in His mercy, it was only seven months. Seven was my number of completion. I found that carrying bitterness and thus having no relationship with the Father was worse than having no children. When I finally gave up the rebellion and repented, our marriage was restored. I finished my year in school and graduated.

My Oil of Myrrh Season

When I graduated from school we were in our seventh year of marriage. This was when God in His sovereign plan allowed us to conceive. However, I soon miscarried that little one. My first thought was God took the baby to punish me for my rebellion. As I read His Word, He assured me that He did not cause the miscarriage, nor was He punishing me. He assured me of His unending love toward me. Then He used this miscarriage for good. He promises to work all things out for the good to those that love Him and to those that are called according to His purpose. (See Romans 8:28.) I knew better than to shake my fist and turn away from God. This time I turned to Him. I ran into His open arms.

Other bitterness and anger towards Him that I still held inside was exposed through this time. The locked doors were opened, and I again could hear His voice and not the voice of lies. The Oil of Myrrh was doing its job. Remember, myrrh was a healing herb that would get the "toxins" out. It was good for healing wounds. I was broken, and the wounds from barrenness and rebellion were about to be healed.

HE HEARS OUR CRY

Shut away in my room, I cried out to the Lord the day I miscarried. He heard me and gave me His promise of being a happy mother of children. I remember laying face first on my bed and sobbing so hard my stomach ached. I had such pain in my heart that I was literally broken-hearted. The Bible says, "He does not forget the cries of the humbled (afflicted)" (Ps. 9:12, NKJV, Destiny Bible). He heard my same cries years before, but this time I turned to my Father as a broken-hearted daughter. Instead of putting my faith in doctors, I put my faith and trust in God and His Word. He hears the cries and comes.

HANNAH WAS ANOTHER BROKEN PRINCESS

In my room, He also revealed to me the story of Hannah, in the book of Samuel. She, too, cried out in her affliction. Hannah also was barren and thusly distraught. In her despair, Hannah cried at the temple before God. Eli, the temple priest, heard her cry. At first he was going to kick her out because he thought she was drunk with wine and babbling funny words. She managed to pull herself together enough to explain to him her despair. Eli blessed her with a prayer that broke off the curse of barrenness. Soon she was with child.

In the story, Hannah had a baby boy and named him Samuel. She dedicated him in the temple for God's purpose. After I read the story, I told the Lord that if I ever conceived again, and if it were a boy, I would name him Samuel. I also told the Lord I would dedicate him to His divine service. The Father was speaking to me loud and clear that day through the Scriptures.

My Time of Spices and Perfume Arrived

One month after the miscarriage, I found out I was once again with child. What a joyful time for Chuck and I. God fulfilled the Word that He gave me out of the story of Hannah. Our son, Samuel John, was born on Oct. 1, 1988. *Samuel* means: "asked of God." *John* means: "God is gracious." We also held up to our promise we made to God. We dedicated Samuel's life to the Lord's service as a newborn. He is already being used mightily for God.

Our Father works in kingdom ways. It usually never makes sense to us, because we are used to the ways of the world. The more you watch and experience His ways, the more you understand His kingdom. Everything is under His hand and care.

When I became pregnant with Samuel, I was filled to the brim with joy, and I was in the season of sweet spices and perfumes.

Exactly two years after Samuel was born, Sophia El-Rae was born on Oct. 2, 1990. Sophia means "wisdom of God." El-Rae mean "noble and doe." Then last, but not least, our little Phoebe Lee was born on May 7, 1993 at 7:00 a.m. With seven being the number of completion, I knew Phoebe was my last baby. She completed our little family. Phoebe means "shining, pure, honest, and true." Lee means "poetic, and from the pasture meadow." God's ways are so awesome! I am a blessed and happy mother, just like He said I would be. My children are such a blessing. They bring me much joy. Do my stories help you understand better the season of myrrh and the season of perfume and spice?

YOU, TOO, WERE BORN FOR SUCH A TIME AS THIS

Like Esther, you were born for such a time as this. Look to the King to see whether you are in the *Oil of Myrrh* season or the *Sweet Spice and Perfume* season. Be at peace, knowing He is at work doing a good work in your life. The Holy Spirit is always available to help you to fulfill your call and destiny. You can even learn to walk in peace and joy during those difficult myrrh seasons. Remember *Princess*; you are in the preparation process down here on this earth to someday meet the King of kings and Lord of lords in the heavenly kingdom. What you learn here has eternal value. You are being shaped for eternity.

Listen and watch for the language of the Father in all areas of your life. Pay attention to details in your life. Walk in divine grace and be brave just like Esther. Always be wise by seeking first His Kingdom, and you, too, will walk in the destiny that your name represents. Your name is ringing forth your destiny. This is the generation that all of the witnesses in heaven are cheering on! There is not another *Princess* like you.

PERSONAL PRINCESS REFLECTIONS

1. List all the activities and clubs you have been, and are presently, in. For which ones do you have a true passion? Why?

2. Look up your first and middle name in name books or on the Internet. What do they mean?

3. Does this surprise you?

4. Have you ever done anything that was beyond your own natural capabilities and it affected a whole group of people for the better?

5. Would you like to do that someday?

6. Does anything stand out now that you could think of doing?

7. Can you relate to the *Oil of Myrrh* and *Oil of Perfume* seasons?

8. What season are you in right now?

9. What do you think God is doing in this season of your life?

10. List one mountaintop experience and one valley experience in your life.

11. How did this chapter apply to your life?

Chapter 7

REST IN YOUR ROYALTY

AS YOU BEGIN to walk the dock of destiny that your name represents, you will face various encounters that will try and steal the peace given to you from your Father. Anything that happens in your life, to the nation, or world, that you can do nothing about, can cause you to question your future and be anxious. Once you begin thinking in that direction, you will soon find yourself tossing and turning like a churning sea.

I have experienced this anxiety a few times since terrorists attacked America on September 11, 2001. I do not think I am alone in those feelings. Recently I lived through four hurricanes, two of which landed in the very city I live in! Even natural disasters can cause anxiety. Unrest and anxiety go hand in hand. These are real feelings that real people deal with every day and everywhere. The remedy for this unrest is not far away. The Lord offers to His children a rest that the world does not know. What is this rest and how do you get it? How do you dump the balled-up knot in your stomach? Read on, *Princess.*

SCHOOL-DAY ANXIETY

Even as a young girl I experienced feelings of unrest and anxiety. Speech class projects were enough to send me over the edge and into the dark cloud of anxiety. Few people would guess that of me, but it was there. Making the due date for a school project, or fretting over try-outs for sports or drama, would almost make me sick at night. I would break out into a cold sweat as a test was placed in front of me on my desk. Watching the news and hearing the conflicts and rumors of war in the world would unsettle me.

Both your generation and mine are dealing with natural disasters, world conflict, war, and terrorism. Fear of the unknown is usually the primary cause of unrest. World conflicts will not go away and seem to grow larger with each day. Living in a state of unrest with no peace is not a life for a *Princess*. Only through the Lord can we find rest.

As an adult, I daily make the decision to choose His rest over anxiousness. In the workplace or in my kitchen, the Bible tells me not to be anxious about anything, but in everything by prayer, petition, and thanksgiving I make my requests known to God. When I do this, the Bible says that the peace of God, which transcends all understanding, will guard my heart and mind in Christ Jesus. (See Philippians 4:6–7.) The pressures and responsibilities of life never end, and only increase with age. Learning to deal with unrest at a young age will be profitable to you.

How we think and what we speak out of our mouths makes all the difference in the world and in the Kingdom. In chapter 8 we will talk about the nine fruits of the Spirit. Self-control is one of the fruits. We have a choice to use self-control in troubled times. If we choose to give into these feelings of unrest rather than listen to what the Word of God says, we easily fall into sin. The unrest proves that you are not looking to God for the outcome, but rather to yourself or others. When you look to yourself and others you are not trusting God. Again, let's look at a picture in the Bible to help us see it is an age-old challenge; God wants us to see the solution.

THE FORTY-YEAR ROAD TRIP

This is the story of Moses. Every year, no matter what, my brother–in-law Daniel has to watch the Hollywood version of this story on TV. It is really an amazing deliverance story. In the story, Pharaoh was the King of Egypt, and at the time of Moses' birth, Pharaoh sent out a decree to throw all newborn Hebrew boys into the Nile River. When Moses was three months old, his mother could no longer hide him from the soldiers. She placed him in a basket and sent him floating down the Nile. She knew the *Princess,* Pharoh's daughter, bathed in the water there and had hopes of Moses being saved from death. Sure enough, when the *Princess* found him she raised this little Hebrew child to be a prince of Egypt. At least, that is what she thought she was doing. All the Hebrew people were Egyptian slaves at this time. Yet, here in the palace, was a Hebrew child. God was up to something. I find it interesting that God used a *Princess* to save Moses from death. Another example of *Princess* Destiny.

Moses' name means "drawn out and born." The *Princess* drew him out of the water, but God later drew him out of Egypt. God ended the prince-grooming season of his life and transported him into the wilderness to learn how to care for sheep. Talk about a career change. Shepherding helped Moses to fulfill his destiny. He was drawn out of Egypt and born of God in the wilderness. Just like his name says. Isn't that cool?

After forty years in the wilderness, God came to Moses

and sent him back to Egypt to free the Hebrew people. So he did. It was not an easy job, but he listened to God, did as he said, and it all worked out. Moses established the Hebrews as an independent nation and prepared them for entrance to the Promised Land. He drew them out of Egypt and a nation was born. Again, just like his name says.

The Hebrew people had been slaves to the Pharaohs of Egypt for 400 years. To leave Egypt and go to their Promised Land was their heart's cry, but to get Egypt out of their systems was another ordeal. What scholars say could have been a three-day journey lasted forty years. Why such a long road trip?

The Exodus Begins

It was a mass exodus out of Egypt for the Hebrew slaves. They were amazed and thankful towards God for their freedom and hope of the Promised Land. They knew they were headed to a land flowing with milk and honey where they could worship God freely. Even those in Egypt who never worshipped the God of Abraham, Isaac, and Jacob left Egypt with them because they saw the power of the Hebrew's God and believed.

Before Pharaoh released the slaves, he needed to be persuaded by God to free them. Pharaoh kept saying "No" to Moses when He would ask for the Hebrew's freedom. God sent plagues, a hailstorm, rivers of blood, killed livestock, sent boils, brought a locust plague, and finally caused the death of each unprotected firstborn son. When Pharaoh's son died he realized that he was no match for God Almighty. He finally let the Hebrew slaves go free. At last they were free to go to their Promised Land.

ROADBLOCKS ARE OPPORTUNITIES TO PERSEVERE

With each request to let his people go, Pharaoh said "No". His denials were used to persuade others to believe in God. Every time Pharaoh said "No" to Moses' demands God would perform another sign and wonder to persuade Pharaoh otherwise. The roadblocks on your dock of destiny will be used in the same manner to lead others to Christ. Do not let roadblocks give you an excuse as to why you are not moving forward into the destiny God has for you. Giving into defeat will steal your peace. No peace is no rest, and a *Princess* cannot live without rest.

Let the roadblocks become a reason to rejoice in being a *Princess*. You are to count it as pure joy whenever you face trials of any kind. Doing this will produce patience in your life. James 1:2–3 says, "My brethren, count it all joy when you fall in various trials, knowing that the testing of your faith produces patience." Others are watching your every move, action, and attitude. Some of the people that left Egypt were not even Hebrews. That is why the Bible calls it a "mixed multitude." They saw God at work. Let others see God at work in you. Look at these trials as new adventures!

MY ROAD BLOCK STORY

I learned about roadblocks on a ministry trip in Germany. I was helping with worship at the "Glory Conference" in Berlin. I was with my ministry friends Karen, Louise, and Betty. (Note: the names have been changed to preserve the anonymity of those involved.)

Louise, Betty, and I were in our hotel room when Carol knocked on the door around midnight. We were given tickets to see President Clinton the next day in Berlin at an airfield celebration. He was in town celebrating the fiftieth anniversary of American's feeding the hungry project at this airfield during World War II. This celebration was sold out, but God gave Sam (one of the conference speakers) favor and led him to the right guy at the right time that night. Sam shared his tickets.

It is not every day you get to see your president face to face. Another adventure was awaiting me. In the morning Louise, Betty, and I rode in the van with Sam and Joan (another conference speaker), and made our way through the streets of Berlin. When we arrived at the airfield, I began to realize what a big event this really was.

We showed our ticket and passport to the police at the gate. Everyone crossed through the gate except for me. The police pulled me aside and began to ask questions. You never know why that stuff happens. I smiled and pretended I understood German. This was the first roadblock of the day. Sam came to my rescue. He said something to the police officer, which seemed to work, and then took me by the hand to join the rest of the group. That was that. It was like something my Dad would have done for me.

Once inside we had to take a transport vehicle over to the celebration area. I could see bleachers as we got off the bus. When I saw the multitudes of people, I doubted we would find a seat. This place was packed. Sam, being the media guy that he is, parted ways with us women and sat with the TV people covering the story.

THE TEA PARTY MANEUVER

Joan asked us to all link hands so we could maneuver through the crowd more effectively. She said, "Just pretend we are at a tea party mingling our way through the crowd." She was not in the *little faith* department like me. She headed toward those bleachers. We weaved our way through the crowd and actually came close enough to see the gate entrance to the bleachers and the airfield. This entrance was heavily guarded by military police. This gate was our passage to the bleachers.

I was the smallest of the group, and on the tail end of our human whip. We weaved in and out of the crowd as far as we could. Finally we came to a stand still in the massive crowd of people. The very tall Germans were beginning to press into me from all sides. I was sweating, hot, and irritated. At that point I cried out, "Jesus, help me!" Nobody even cared that I was screaming like a lunatic. Louise heard me, but she just laughed. I know she was starting to lose it herself. We were both ready to give up and go back to the hotel. But not Joan. She knew something we did not.

Just when you are about to give up, God will send a deliverer. A German man came along, pushing and prodding his way past us. Louise and I thought he was rude as he went by. When he was next to Joan he said, "Excuse me." Joan said, "I will excuse you if you remember me up at the gate. I must get through and sit down." He nodded his head and went past. Minutes later we saw him standing next to a police officer, looking our way. Soon after, he waved to Joan and yelled, "How many in your group?" She yelled back, "Four!" Her hand was raised and four fingers were pointing up to heaven. With that, the police officer said to the crowd, "Let these people through."

PARTING OF THE SEA

It was like Moses parting the Red Sea. The crowd separated, and we walked to the front and through the gate. I even had a man ask me if he could pretend to be part of our party! This roadblock proved to be nothing. And to think I was ready to give up—what a wimp! This special treatment somehow gave people the idea that we were important. Which, in some ways, we were. Being daughters of the Most High God has its privileges! These *Princesses* needed a seat! We were on another learning lesson about faith, roadblocks, and not giving up.

Once through the gate, we were seated in the second row with the White House Press. I recognized many of the TV reporters sitting there from CNN. We were only a few feet away from the President as he walked by. Although I did not agree with many things President Clinton represented during his time in office, it was an honor to see him. I also knew enough that God has called us to pray for those in authority over us that day, including government officials with whom we do not see eye to eye. I gained an appreciation for our American government; I walked away more patriotic.

I know it was not a surprise to Joan, where we ended up sitting. She saw it long before the day began. She probably saw herself sitting right there the night before as she was handed a ticket. She believed, and pursued through all the roadblocks. She never once grumbled or complained. I was taught a valuable lesson in life. Never give up. All things are possible, if you believe.

What Is Wrong With These People?

The Hebrew slaves also had many roadblocks while waiting for Pharaoh's release. They watched God Almighty do spectacular miracles to get Pharaoh to let the people go. Then, once Pharaoh released them, they again saw some roadblocks on their way to the Promised Land. The roadblocks were there to actually help the Hebrews grow in their faith and trust in God.

Their first roadblock was the Red Sea. It was massive,

but not for God! He just split it apart so they could cross. He gave them a pillar of fire at night so they could see, and a cloud of glory to follow by day. He sent fresh bread to eat every morning, and poured water out of a rock to drink. Wow! With those kinds of signs and wonders, wouldn't you feel like you could totally trust in this wonderful God? Roadblocks can actually be quite adventurous, and they do not need to steal your peace.

However, the huge group that followed Moses through the desert grumbled and complained non-stop. They were constantly murmuring to one another saying, "We need food like we had in Egypt. We want onions, leeks, fruits and vegetables...give us more water, we are way too thirsty, this trip is too long, where is the meat?" (Num. 11:5; Exod. 15:24, 16:3, nkjv, author's paraphrase). They even complained about Moses' leadership skills. Can you believe it? God Almighty picked him to be the leader, and they still were not satisfied. Go figure. But that is exactly what anxiety will try to do to you. It is what people sink into rather quickly.

WE MUST REST TO ENTER OUR PROMISED LAND

The Hebrews did not remember the promises God had given to them. You, too, have promises from God for your life. The Bible is full of these promises. As you live out your destiny these promises unfold on your dock of life.

The Hebrews were official navel gazers. They complained so much that finally God said, "I will not let these people go into the Promised Land because they did not rest in me." Whoa! Did He say rest? Yes, in this reference rest means: trusting and obeying with your heart, mind, and soul. It is important to learn this principle of resting in the Father and His promises for you.

You can fall into this trap of unbelief, mistrust, and disobedience although you know God is quite big enough to handle your problems. Looking no farther than yourself for answers and being consumed by your circumstances you will act like the Hebrews. A whole generation of Hebrews was denied entrance to the Promised Land because of their disobedience and lack of trust in God. It took forty years before any of the Hebrews entered the Promised Land. God wanted all the grumblers and complainers to die. Those who entered were free from the sin of their elders before them.

Dump the Baggage— It Weighs Down Your Dock

When you are about to enter a new phase of your destiny with the King, you do not want old baggage, old patterns, and old habits to follow you. You have a promised destiny here on earth, and there are many phases to this destiny. The minute you become a believer you are walking on the dock of your destiny. You may not think so, but you are. Each phase is an exciting part of His plan for your life. Learn as much as you can in each phase, and leave behind the things He tells you to discard. Our final resting-place is the New Heaven and New Earth that John the Apostle saw and wrote about in the book of Revelation. He wrote that this Heaven is our eternal Promised Land where we will rule and reign over nations and cities.

Fear Will Try to Block You

Fear will try to block you from moving forward on your dock of destiny. It is usually when you are unsure of the future that you allow fear to block you. When I was stuck in the middle of all the tall Germans and sweating like a pig, I wanted to give up. My peace left and everything closed in on me. Since then, when I begin feeling like this, I just say, "Oh God, help me!" He loves it when we cry out to Him for help. He is such an awesome Father!

First John 4:18 says, "There is no fear in love; but perfect love casts out fear." God's love is the only perfect love you will ever know. You will truly rest in Him when you know and understand the full measure of love that your Father has for you. When you rest in Him you are saying you trust Him. When you trust Him, you obey Him and His commandments. When you obey Him, you are telling Him you love Him. You will then begin to recognize that you are no longer held back by fear as you start to experience more depths of His love. His love paralyzes fear.

LET IT FLOW

Kingdom life is all about His love flowing in us and through us. This is the love that the world around us needs to experience. It can only come through earthen vessels (people) willing to let it flow through them. Fear will have no place in us when we understand this and experience it. The Father is always stretching us and challenging us to trust Him and obey Him.

Fear paralyzed the Hebrews in the desert. Their old ways of thinking and patterns of living began to overtake them. Fear crept in and they tried to handle things on their own because they were afraid of the future. Rather than remembering and giving thanks to God for all He had done in the past, they grumbled about their future. Think about that one.

Walking the same old way will never work when you begin to move in a new direction. Isn't that the truth? When you fear the outcome of a situation and wonder about its effect, you will automatically fall back into old ways to protect yourself from being hurt. This will always cause you to retreat instead of advance. I wrote a song called "Empty Me" that says, "I am going to take root downward, bear fruit upward, advance forward, and move on toward eternity." When you take root in Him you will always advance and bear fruit.

Remember, fear creeps in when you are not sure of the outcome. However, if the Father is saying, "Trust me," then who better is there to trust than Him? That is a total no-brainer. To survive the times you are now living in, you must trust and obey His commands at every turn in the road of your life. Not only for your benefit, but for others, too. When you trust and obey, He promises us rest. This rest will truly be upon you, and nothing will stop you from entering His plans for your life.

Learn Your Lesson and Get Out!

The Hebrews walked in circles while in the desert. Walking in circles in a spiritual desert is a drag. Trust me, I have been there many times. A good rule of thumb is, "No grumbling or complaining" when you are in a desert time. It will only cause the trip to be delayed, or worse yet, you will not make it to the destiny God has for you.

The Hebrews had many fears, many complaints, and many setbacks because of their grumbling and complaining to God. It was His mercy that was keeping them in the desert to help clean out the residue left over from Egypt. God kept giving them chances to trust and obey Him. They just kept blowing it.

Desert Time

So what exactly is desert time anyway? Desert time is what you get when you grumble and complain during a test or trial in your life. When you fail to keep your mouth shut

you will forfeit your peace automatically. No pressure—no time! If you have not learned about already, the desert is not a pleasant place to live. It is hot, dry and uncomfortable.

Patience, faithfulness and trust given to you for purification will keep you out of the desert experience. So try and pass your tests and trials the first time. If you can have joy in the midst of a trial, you have learned one of life's biggest lessons on true rest.

The desert experience can help you grow by leaps and bounds—so grow and get out. It is a thirsty, dry place. Find your oasis in Him!

WAKE UP AND SMELL THE COFFEE

As a princess, we are capable of many feelings. Some are good and some are bad. We must choose to pick the good over the bad. I finally woke up and smelled the coffee on this revelation. I began to understand that God actually allows situations to take place to remove the habit of grumbling and complaining out of my life. So I said to myself, "Why grumble and complain? The Bible tells me to give thanks in all things." He is God and I am not. Acting like a child of the King is being obedient and trusting in Him. It is that simple. Do not be like Pharaoh. It took the death of his son to arrive at that revelation!

Stinking thinking and handling situations poorly will get you another one-way ticket to the desert. Why go there? He has such wonderful things in store for you. He does not want you in the desert. However, He will allow you to stay there until you learn what you need to learn.

RESTING AND TRUSTING ARE THE SAME

Some of the Israelites blew their chance to live in the Promised Land because they did not trust God. R you will forfeit your peace automatically. No peace—no fun. If you have not figured it out already, the desert is not a pleasant place to live. It is hot, dry, and uncomfortable.

Passing the tests and trials given to you for purification will keep you out of the desert experience. So try and pass your tests and trials the first time. If you can have joy in the midst of a trial, you have learned one of life's biggest lessons on true rest.

The desert experience can help you grow by leaps and bounds—so grow and get out! It is a thirsty, dry place—find your oasis in Him!

WAKE UP AND SMELL THE COFFEE

As a *Princess,* we are capable of many feelings. Some are good and some are bad. We must choose to pick the good over the bad. I finally woke up and smelled the coffee on this revelation. I began to understand that God actually allows situations to take place to remove the habitual grumbling and complaining out of my life. So I said to myself, "Why grumble and complain? The Bible tells me to give thanks in all things." He is God and I am not. Acting like a child of the King is being obedient and trusting in Him. It is that simple. Do not be like Pharaoh. It took the death of his son to arrive at that revelation.

Seeing, thinking, and handling situations poorly will buy you another one-way ticket to the desert. Why go there? He has such wonderful things in store for you. He does not want you in the desert. However, He will allow you to stay there until you learn what you need to learn.

RESTING AND TRUSTING ARE THE SAME

Some of the Israelites blew their chance to live in the Promised Land, because they did not trust God. Resting and trusting are the same. When you trust, you let go. When you let go, you are flooded with peace and joy, which ultimately is His rest. So until they trusted Him, God had them go around and around and around in the wilderness. It took a whole new generation to get the picture. You are a new generation. Get this picture while you are young, and see how far He will take you in His Kingdom!

He does this because of His mercy on your life. He does not want you bound up with jealousy, fear, anger, boastfulness, pride, hatred, grumbling, complaining, and every other curse. He wants to give you good things. He wants you free from those things that so easily entangle you. It pleases the Father to give you, His daughter and *Princess,* the gifts of the Kingdom. Every good and perfect gift comes from our Father. He loves to watch you walk into all the phases of the destiny He alone created for you.

Being a Princess in the Promised Land

I have found that the more I read, speak, and meditate on the word of God, the more freedom I get in all these areas. We will always be tempted down here on earth with these carnal feelings and thoughts, especially with all we are now experiencing with our world and war. There is always something to complain about, and there is always a situation in which it is difficult to trust God. As a *Princess* you do not have to live in that carnal earthly kingdom, you belong to the Kingdom of God. Climb up higher to your royal calling.

Take an Evaluation

Got peace? Got joy? All knotted up? These are good barometers for you to use. If you are missing joy and peace in your life, stop what you are doing and evaluate what you have been saying, doing, and thinking. The Bible says even our thoughts are heard by the Lord. He hears and sees the intentions and motives of our hearts.

One huge thing I have learned over the years was to have His Word come out of my mouth and then to try to live what it says. This has protected me and helped me to continue on to the next phases of my destiny that He created just for me. I have actually read through the Bible and wrote out scriptures I want applied in my daily life. Then I apply it personally to me.

READ THE WORD

I believe the Word of God will impart life into you, if you learn to use it, believe it, and live it. His Word is truth, and if you know the truth, it will set you free. (See John 8:32.) We all need freedom from bad attitudes, bad thoughts, and curses to fulfill our destiny. He wants a clean vessel to work through. Reading the Word renews, cleanses, and strengthens our spirit, body, and soul.

From Joyce Meyers' book, Me and My Big Mouth,[1] I copied some of her paraphrases of scriptures that she suggested her readers memorize. I stuck them on a little notebook that I fit into my purse. I personalized them so I was speaking the truth to myself. I have listed some of these below. Go ahead and give it a try; say them out loud. You will see what I mean. It is amazing. It feels good to speak truth over your life.

- "I am always a positive encourager. I edify and build up; I never tear down or destroy" (Rom. 15:2).

- "I can do all things through Christ who strengthens me" (Phil. 4:13).

- "I cry to God most High Who performs on my behalf and rewards me" (2 Chron. 16:9).
- "I am righteous through Christ, therefore, I am as bold as a lion" (Prov. 28:1).
- "Grace is upon my lips and mercy is in my heart and you will bring me before kings" (Prov. 16:13).
- "I am aglow and burning with the spirit" (Rom. 12:11).
- "I fear no evil for You are with me" (Ps. 23:4).
- "I am forgetting what lies behind, and pressing forward to what lies ahead" (Phil. 3:14).
- "I know God's voice, and I always obey what He tells me" (John 10:3–5, 14–16, 27; 14:15).
- "I humble myself and God exalts me" (1 Pet. 5:6).
- "Let the words of my mouth and the meditation of my heart be acceptable in your sight; Oh Lord my rock and redeemer" (Ps. 19:14).
- I do not hate, or walk in unforgivness (1 John 2:11; Eph. 4:32).

Meditate on Him and His Word

When I first began this process, I would read my personal scriptures, sometimes twice a day. Now I have them in my heart and daily remember them when I need them. I still read them from time to time. I find new ones every time I read the Bible. Now I read a scripture out loud just like a prayer with someone's name or mine put into it.

Let the Holy Spirit guide you as you pick out your *Princess* scriptures. You will find that our gracious King and Lord will fulfill those very words coming out of your mouth. Remember that the King's word cannot come back without accomplishing its goal. His words never come back void.

Each phase of this unfolding destiny has been a blast. Getting there has not always been such a blast, but that is my own fault. Once I turn my eyes back to Him, it is a blast again. Keep your eyes on the King and you will do all that has been planned for you. It is a high price to pay. It will cost you everything, but it is worth everything. Let His Word walk you down the dock of your destiny.

OUR ETERNAL PROMISED LAND

Well *Princess,* I hope you were encouraged to continue to press on toward our eternal Promised Land: the New Heaven and the New Earth. This is when we will hear our Father say to us, "Well done my good and faithful servant." (See Matthew 25:21.) This is our Hope of Glory.

Hold true to the teachings of Christ and continue to walk the dock. You are a special *Princess* and are truly loved. Love, listen, and obey the King and you will live in safety and fulfill your destiny while here on earth! Envision Moses and the Israelites roaming around in circles. This is an awesome word picture to help us all stay out of the desert, and remain at the King's banquet table in righteousness, peace, and joy!

Love and forgive through the Son and you will live in peace,
Trust and Rest in the King and you will live in joy.
Righteousness, Peace, and Joy—that's the Kingdom of God.

—ROBIN RINKE

Personal Princess Reflections

1. What situations seem to steal your peace?
2. What does resting in the Lord mean to you?
3. What will give you a one-way ticket to the desert?
4. What will cause you to stay in the desert?
5. What is the first thing you should do when you no longer sense peace or joy in your life?
6. What can the Word of God do for you? Share one personal verse you have found and will use.
7. What did this chapter mean to you?

Chapter 8

PRINCESS KEY #1: GUARDING YOUR HEART

IN THE NEXT three chapters I cover three important keys you will need for this Kingdom life as a *Princess*. Key number one is: *Guarding Your Heart.*

WARNING: WET DOCK AHEAD

At our lake home in summer, my mom would caution us kids about running on the slippery wooden dock after a rainstorm. Wooden docks can get slimy when they soak up a lot of water.

Just like my mother's warning of the slippery dock, we too, as daughters of the King, should heed warnings from the Bible. In doing so we will not fall and slip off our dock of destiny with the Lord. In Proverbs 4:23 (amp) it says, "Keep and guard your heart with all vigilance and above all that you guard, for out of it flow the springs of life."

Above all? We need to guard? Wow, this must be important. This means that we need to guard or protect our hearts twenty-four hours a day, seven days a week, 365 days a year. Why all the fuss? The Father knows when we let down our guard our hearts get wounded, dirty, and filled with the world. When that happens our springs of life can rapidly become sewers of death. He loves us and wants to protect us so He warns us in advance.

Springs of Life Are Worth Guarding

What are the springs of life, and why should I guard them? Jesus is the living water that flows out of us. He is the spring of life. Jesus lives in us through His Holy Spirit. That is the reason why we are to protect our hearts by guarding them. We do not want this spring to be plugged or polluted by the world. As His *Princess,* these springs of life will supernaturally flow out of us because we have the Kingdom of God within us. This is worth guarding.

When He flows out of us, through the Holy Spirit, the nine fruits of the Spirit are visible for others to see. These fruits will draw those around us to the spring for refreshing water. This water will satisfy forever. Rivers of living water should flow out of us. You will know Jesus is flowing freely when the precious fruit of the Spirit is evident.

The Nine Fruits of the Spirit Are Worth Guarding

The nine fruits of the spirit are as follows: righteousness, peace, joy, patience, longsuffering, love, kindness, mercy, and faithfulness. You will find that in Galatians 5:22. These fruits should be evident in all of the Father's children, big or small. Some fruits are more evident in your life than others. Joy flows from me much easier than longsuffering. Guess which one the Father is always working on with me? Yep, looooooongsuffering.

Apples grow on apple trees when they are properly nourished, watered, and cared for. The nine fruits of the Spirit grow in the children of God if they are properly nourished by the Word, watered by the Holy Spirit, and cared for by the Father. These are the good fruits, unlike the fruit produced by weeds that we studied earlier. When you learn how to properly guard your heart, you will see how it protects the fruit of the Spirit from becoming rotten!

When others inspect you, do they see the fruits of the Spirit growing in and on you? Can they tell you are a child of the kingdom of God marked by the kind of fruit you are producing? More importantly, what does the Father see?

THE BIG MOUTH FROM TOKYO

I was in the Tokyo Airport waiting for my plane home from a two-week ministry trip. I was exhausted and just wanted to be left alone to read my book and sleep. I prayed for the seat next to me on the flight home to be empty so I could curl up in a little ball after dinner and sleep for eight hours. Little did I know about the "Big Mouth" I was about to meet.

I was minding my own business, quietly reading, when I was rudely interrupted by a loud voice asking me, "So, where are you going?" I hesitated in responding because I did not want to get involved in a conversation. I was extremely exhausted and not feeling social at all! Besides, could he not see I was reading a book? I hesitated and then looked over my book and said, "I am going home to Minnesota." Hoping that was enough of a response, I pulled my book back up over my eyes and returned to my reading.

He continued, "Minnesota! Wow, I am from Chicago. What were you doing in Japan?" In my mind I whipped up several responses to give him that just might shut him up and cause him to leave me alone. However, the Holy

Spirit convicted me in my heart of being a snob. I died to my flesh, put my book down, and said, "I was on a two-week ministry trip and I apologize for being unsocial. I am very tired" With that he exclaimed, "A missionary! You're a missionary? I've never met a missionary before!" Mind you, we were in Asia, and Asians generally do not speak louder than a whisper. They are kind and quiet people. Many of these kind, quiet people were now starring at Mr. Big Mouth and I.

I proceeded to tell him about the trip and answered many of his questions. He was an older gentleman with lots of energy and a bright smile. Soon our flight was called and we stood in line to board the plane. As I waited, I was hoping God made all the arrangements necessary for me that I had prayed about earlier.

Sure enough, God came through! Nobody was sitting next to me when the doors to the plane closed. At least that was the case right up until I snapped my seat belt shut. I then heard, "Robin, hey Robin!" Did I dare look? Did I dare answer? It was Mr. Big Mouth calling my name. I prayed, "Oh Lord, do you really want me to answer back?" I felt in my heart that I was to answer him. So I stood up and went back to see what the fuss was all about. Mr. Big Mouth was sitting in the back middle section of the plane. He smiled brightly as I approached his seat.

He pointed to a young man next to him and said, "Robin, I told this guy you are a missionary and I asked him if he would trade seats with you so you could sleep on your way home; he said he would. That means you could have these three seats and I will also give you mine." I was shocked! Nobody had ever done that for me. I thanked the young man and Mr. Big Mouth for their generosity. It was almost like flying first class! Well, sort of.

GOOD NIGHT—GOOD MORNING!

Mr. Big Mouth and I ate our dinner and chatted about his work in Japan. He then found me many blankets and pillows to make my bed. Soon I was off into la-la land.

Seven hours later I awoke. Mr. Big Mouth, or should I say "Mike," as I had finally gotten his name, offered me a cup of coffee and proceeded to tell me how long I slept. After I brushed my teeth and washed my face, I ate breakfast. Only one more hour to go and we would land in Chicago.

After our breakfast trays were cleared, Mike slapped his hand on the seat's arm rest and said, "Robin, you are just so good, good, good!" His voice was just as loud and energetic as ever. With that comment I looked at him and replied, "It is not me that you see that is good. That is the Lord Jesus in me. Nothing in me is good except Him." He then crossed his arms and said, "Tell me more about this Jesus." Right at that moment the light went on as to why I was sitting where I was sitting. I proceeded in telling him how much God the Father loved him and that His Son Jesus made the way to a right relationship with Him. I shared with Him how he too could have a right relationship with the Father.

I noticed that every word I spoke, Mike would repeat. He not only repeated it, but he repeated it loudly and with excitement. Those around us could hear everything I said about salvation because he would blast it right back to me. I could not have hand picked a better preacher than this! It was at this point that I put two and two together and saw just what the Lord was doing. God had set up this scenario way back in Tokyo.

Let me explain. On the very end of my row was an Orthodox Jewish man quietly reading the paper. Orthodox Jews do not believe that Jesus Christ was, or is, or ever will be, the Messiah. Many of them have never even read the New Testament. That day he, and everyone else on that end of the plane, heard the Gospel message of Jesus Christ, the long awaited Messiah, through the mouth of Mike.

The funny thing about him was he was reading a book called *The Diary of a Jewish Woman*. I thought, *Why would an Irish Catholic man from Chicago be reading a book about Jews?* Of all the books to be reading! I believe I was at the right place at the right time. What God set up I almost missed because of my flesh being tired. Jew or Gentile, God wants all to know about His love.

When we reached Chicago, he helped me with my heavy luggage, found me a cart, and made sure I got through the customs checkpoint. At customs check we each went into different lines. I guess I just expected him to come out of his line at the same time as me. However, that was not the case. I never saw him again. We never even said good-bye.

This Was a Divine Appointment

I could have missed that divine appointment had I not put the book down in Tokyo. The Spirit of the Lord had a plan and it was up to me to walk in love and obedience to fulfill that plan. Many people ate from the fruit of the Spirit that was within me. I will never forget Mike, God's secret agent.

Your Body, Soul, and Spirit Are Worth Guarding

As a *Princess* in the kingdom, we must guard this priceless treasure we have within us. We must protect and grow these nine fruits to maturity so others, like Mike, can eat from our lives. Watching what you let into your heart is key. You are made up of body, soul, and spirit. Each of these areas must be guarded. (See 1 Thessalonians 5:23, AMP.)

- Body: Our physical earthly container
- Soul: Our mind, will, and emotions
- Spirit: Our inner man, or in our case, our "inner *princess*"

Your spirit is where the kingdom of God is housed. The Father's House! Your spirit remains in the kingdom and never dies. Kingdom life is eternal.

Your spirit is affected by everything that passes through your spirit, body, and soul. You are either affected for the good or for the bad; for the positive or negative. We can produce healthy fruits of the Spirit or produce rotten fruit. Guarding your spirit, body, and soul, is a key to staying firmly on the dock and aids you from not falling. Rotten fruit causes you to slip and fall off the dock. When off the dock, your destiny is on hold.

> Guard over your hearts and minds in Christ Jesus. For the rest, brethren, whatever is true, whatever is worthy of reverence and is honorable and seemly, whatever is just, whatever is pure, whatever is lovely and lovable, whatever is kind and winsome and gracious, if there is any virtue and excellence, if there is anything worthy of praise, think on and weigh and take account of these things.
>
> —PHILIPPIANS 4:7–8, AUTHOR'S PARAPHRASE

That passage says it all. It is the perfect measuring stick as to whether something is good or bad for you.

Being Discipled Helps You Guard

I had slippery times during my teen years with my relationship to Jesus. I fell off the dock and into the water, so to speak, many times. Both you and the Lord hurt when you slip and fall. Thinking and then acting on negative thoughts, listening to negative talk and agreeing with it, listening and participating in gossip, and watching things that were not pure affected me and caused me to slip and fall off the dock. I believe a lot of this "falling off the dock" stuff could have been avoided if I would have been taught about the kingdom.

I did not have anyone to disciple (teach) me the first two years of my new kingdom life. I really did not know how to live in the Kingdom of God. Who would? His kingdom is different than this world. We need to be taught so many things. Weekly Bible studies, worship and prayer meetings, attending Bible School, and other resources help you mature so you can produce healthy kingdom fruit.

I knew enough to read my Bible and that it was good, but I also remember having so many questions, but no one to answer them. Asking the Father for wisdom was not even in my vocabulary. I had no one to teach me this truth. I did not yet realize the effect bad choices ultimately had on the kingdom of God that was now inside of me. Having someone or some group to grow with is critical. They can share insights with you and help you in your walk. This book is a type of discipleship. You are learning more about doing things His way and are hopefully growing and maturing from it. There are many ways of being discipled.

A Few Good Mamma Mentors

Having a mentor in your life is also a type of discipleship. I am thankful for my Mother. She has mentored me all of my life. As far as I am concerned, she is the best Mother in the universe. I realize this is not a typical situation. If your situation is different, let me encourage you by saying that the Lord will not leave you Motherless. He knows your every need even before you ask Him. He will bring "Mothers" to you from the family of God when you need them.

I have had the awesome privilege of being mentored by a few strong women of God. This level of discipleship began when Freebird Ministries was coming forth. I did not need to go on a mentor search, and neither will you. The Lord placed each of these mentors in my life at strategic times for His plans and purposes to be fulfilled. Carol Bo Howell, Dawn Lundgren and Linda Rios Brook have all influenced me in many different ways to develop me as a woman of God. Each of them has imparted into me the different things necessary to be a woman in ministry. The Father knows who to bring your way for your walk on the dock. Keep your eyes open for them. They are a gift.

Like Mother, Like Daughter

One day when my daughter, Phoebe, was four years old, I was putting a load of clothes in the washer. She watched me strip down to my undies and bra and throw my clothes in the washer. I was heading upstairs to take a shower when my son's dirty bathroom floor stopped me in my tracks. I cleaned the floor and also noticed the toilet needed a scrubbing too. So out came the cleanser and toilet brush. When I was finished, Phoebe asked me if she could clean the toilet in her bathroom. I told her she could and gave her a few tips on cleaning around the rim. With that she darted up the stairs.

When I peeked in on her to see how she was doing I saw her standing there in her underwear scrubbing the toilet. I said, "Phoebe, why did you take your clothes off?" She looked at me as if puzzled and said, "Momma, this is how you clean toilets!" So there you go—mentor's work!

GET HOOKED UP WITH MATURE FOLLOWERS OF CHRIST

At fourteen the only other Christian believer I knew was my Prep-School roommate, Susan. She was my first convert. She was so excited to hear that Jesus loved her and had a plan for her life that she gladly turned to Him and became a *Princess.* She came from a broken home, and we met at boarding school. I remember sitting there on her yellow bedspread in our dorm room and telling her about my experience with Jesus at camp. She cried and I cried, and we were instantly bonded as sisters that day in a spiritual way. There we were, two little *Princesses,* trying to figure out the kingdom of God on our own. We had no one holding us accountable to grow and live like a *Princess.* This happens all too often, and is a tragedy. We must first learn to be disciples, then disciple others. Actually, this is what grew the early church to its fullness.

Learning to guard your heart starts with asking yourself some pointed questions about your relationships and being honest with the answer. Hanging around the wrong friends seemed to drag me off the dock faster than anything at that particular time in my life. I always knew who the wrong friends were because they did things I did not really want to do, and spoke in ways I did not really want to speak. I should have asked myself, "Are these friends encouraging me in my walk on the dock with Jesus?" This question would have helped me to stay away from relationships that influenced me in the opposite direction of Jesus.

GODLY FRIENDSHIPS HELP YOU REMAIN STRONG

Your closest relationships should always be with strong followers of Christ. Knowing your weaknesses will help you determine what relationships you should pursue to be your *closer* relationships. Your friends' strengths should help you through your weakness, not make them weaker!

Here are a few good questions to ask yourself when deciding about which friends you should spend most of your time with:

1. Is *your* life influencing these friends to the Father and His kingdom?

2. Are *they* influencing you towards the Father and His kingdom?

These two questions can be used in relationships with either boys or girls. If we choose not to use these questions and lie to ourselves about certain relationships that truly are a bad influence, the fruit will begin to show up in your spiritual life. These questions never fail if you are honest with yourself. Your walk on the dock will eventually be interrupted by a splash in the lake. Lies are exposed in time, so you might as well be honest with yourself from the start.

As a *Princess*-in-the-making, use wisdom to choose friends because they will greatly influence that process. Wise choices in friendships keep you from falling off the dock. Right friends will actually help you stay on the dock and will influence the rest of your life.

Remember my friend Lisa from camp? She was a wise choice in friends. She was stable and level-headed. She also was one not to bend to the negative influence of others. This was good for me to see and be around. I always looked up to her; she influenced me towards the kingdom of God not away from it. I learned a lot about respecting myself from her too. These friends are gifts. Sometimes they are in your life for only a season, so cherish them.

In the book of Proverbs it says, "Hang around wise people and you will become wise, hang around with fools and you will become a fool" (Prov. 13:20, amp, author's paraphrase). That is a clear word. You become like those you hang around. Trust me, every part of God's Word is true. Do not prejudge who will be your friends by their outside looks; in doing this you may miss out on some of the most precious relationships you will ever know. I have seen some fancy dressed fools in my day. Look around you and see who the Father has given you as a gift to be your friends. You might be surprised by the package they come in.

My strongest relationships have been with those sisters I connect with in the Spirit and maybe not so much the natural. Praying, worshipping, and talking about God deepens a relationship faster than anything on earth. Daughters of the King are specially marked. Look for those markings. Once you bond in the spirit, you will be friends for eternity. Eternal friendships are precious and help you guard your heart.

Being Obedient Guards Your Heart From Rebellion

Disobedience is called rebellion. The Bible clearly warns in 1 Samuel 15:23 that "Rebellion is as the sin of witchcraft..." If you find yourself trying to manipulate and control things and people to have your own way, you need to take a deep look at your motives and do a heart check. That is rebellion and is witchcraft. We have a very special role as a daughter of the Most High King. Do not pollute the spring of life with rebellion. To sabotage your title of *Princess* with a spirit of rebellion is not worth it.

There really is safety in obedience. Disobedience to God and His Word is rebellion and this will always cause us to fall off the dock. Rebellion is sin. Sin separates us from the Father and leaves a feeling of emptiness inside. The empty feeling may not hit you right away but eventually it catches up with you.

Secular books and movies now circulating the globe are trying to make witchcraft a household word. Do not go there *Princess*! It has always been and always will be an abomination to the Father to even look at anything that has to do with witchcraft. Evil is evil no matter how cute and alluring the package is made to market it.

DO NOT BE CHARMED BY THE OCCULT

Witchcraft is defined as "the power, practices, or art of witches; sorcery; enchantments; attraction or charm" (from www.dictionary.com, August 2004). The definition of a witch is so opposite of a *Princess.* Do not be charmed or bewitched into the evil influence of casting spells or anything else you might have heard. Moviemakers and authors are working overtime to come up with new ways to influence your generation to taste and then get hooked in this evil craft. Do not be misled. It may look innocent, but it is not. It is all part of an evil plot of the devil to entrap you and knock you off of the destiny God has for you.

Ouji boards, horoscopes, palm reading, magic eight balls, levitation, séances, fantasy role playing games, psychics, voodoo, tarot cards, Wicca, and other false religions are all part of this demonic realm. This is only a few of them. If you open yourself up to this realm, you will shut off the flow of God in your life.

If you have participated in any of the above you need to come clean. I participated in many stupid things as a kid at slumber parties. I had no idea I was participating in what the Bible calls sorcery, and neither did my friends. That is exactly the enemy's intent. Opening doors to the demonic realm is not a game.

After I became a *Princess*, I heard messages from various preachers on this topic. I found myself needing to shut some doors that I had opened innocently. Read Galatians 5:19 through 21. This passage clearly states that those involved in sorcery will not inherit the kingdom of God. The depth of your involvement will determine the depth of the stronghold made in your life. I repented and then renounced those past hidden things done in secret. You can do that yourself. Depending upon your involvement, you may need further counseling to help you shut those doors. Your pastor can direct you in this service.

STAY ON THE DRY DOCK

On the dry, secure dock is where you will be most at peace with your heavenly Father, yourself, and others. This is also where you will walk in the greatest joy. Maybe you can relate to the falling off the dock deal. Jesus is always there ready to lift us up out of the water and onto the dock again. He lifts us up and out of the slimy clay and sets our feet on the rock to stay.

It can be a humbling thing to slip away from Him and fall in the water. For me it was humbling to have friends watch as I got back up out of the water. I was always especially humbled in front of the friends that I had witnessed to about the kingdom of God. A dripping wet *Princess*, with eyeliner streaming down her cheeks, can be quite a sight. I would always feel like a hypocrite, and rightly so, because that is exactly what I was.

When we stumble and fall, we cause others that are watching us do the same. Causing a sister or brother in the kingdom to stumble because of your rebellion does not please the King. Also, causing a nonbeliever to be turned off about this kingdom stuff does not please the King, either. We must keep in mind that our actions do have eternal consequences.

This world has seen enough hypocrites from the church. It is up to us to change that by living like kingdom *Princesses* and not like rebellious, worldly children. Being honest with others is the best policy whenever you blow your witness and fall off the dock.

GUARD YOUR PRINCESS IDENTITY

It is important to protect and guard this identity you receive as a *Princess*. Your reputation is like gold. Remember that the devil is always looking for ways to steal this *Princess* title from you. His main goal is to stop you from moving ahead and walking in your destiny. When you are walking in your destiny, you are a threat to his ugly kingdom of darkness.

Maybe you think this guarding is a lot of work. It can be in one sense, but in another sense it can be boiled down to one thing: love. The first and foremost destiny to fulfill, as a *Princess* in the kingdom of God is to, "Love the Lord your God with all your heart, and with all your soul, with all your strength, and with all your mind, and your neighbor as yourself." That is from Luke 10:27 (NIV).

Love never fails. If something fails it was not wrapped

in love. To love Him is to spend time with Him, and then in return He can fill you with more of His love. His love always draws others to the Kingdom. When that love fills your heart, the springs of life will overflow to others. Rebellion will have no room to operate when love is freely flowing.

USING THE FIRST KEY

In review, to guard your heart, in essence, means three things:

1. Become a disciple of Jesus' teachings. (Having a mentor helps.)
2. Make right relationships.
3. Walk in obedience to the Father.

Follow these instructions and you will own the first key of guarding your heart.

PRINCESS REFLECTIONS

1. What is the first key to help you stay on the dock walking in your destiny?
2. Who is the "Spring of Life" in you?
3. List the nine fruits of the spirit.
4. Do you allow things into your body, soul, and spirit that affect you negatively? List those things.
5. Do you have anyone holding you accountable for your actions?

6. Are you being discipled in your walk? If not, where could you go?

7. Do you attract right relationships, or are you a magnet for bad influences?

8. What does the Bible call rebellion? (It starts with a W...)

9. The world is buying the lie that witchcraft is cute and harmless. Are you? Ask for prayer if you need it.

10. What was the main thing you got out of this chapter?

Chapter 9

Princess Key #2: Repentance

Rain is not the only element that can make a dock slippery. Bird droppings can be just as much of a culprit. It is slimy stuff and easy to slip on. Being wise and watchful is a necessary tool to avoid its trap. Who, in her right mind, would want to purposely step in bird droppings? Doing so could land you in the lake.

Repent From Sin—Duh!

Going back and committing the same sin time and time again is like seeing bird droppings on the dock and purposely stepping in it knowing full well you just might slip and fall off the dock.

Romans 6:1 says, "Shall we continue in sin that grace may abound?" No! Just because you know you can repent and be cleansed from your sin is no reason to continue to sin. Eventually it will catch up to you. The consequences of sin are death. Eventually death will come. Spiritual, mental, or even possibly physical death can and will happen. Do not play with sin. Be quick to repent. Change your way of thinking. That means to turn from the thing that separated you from God and never go back.

As long as you are alert, alive, and breathing, it is never too late to repent with the Father. You are still His *Princess* even when you are all wet from the fall into the lake due to sin. Your Father sees you and loves you. He has promised to never leave you or forsake you. Just tell Him you are sorry. He loves you so much, and will open His arms to you and restore your broken relationship.

Asking for His forgiveness automatically extends Jesus' hand out to you so you can get out of the water and back on the dock. Quick repentance is the key to getting back on the dock once you have slipped. The faster you get out, the faster you will dry off. Then the faster you dry off, the faster you can continue your walk down the dock for His kingdom purposes to be fulfilled.

THE FLESH IS WEAK

My heart always wants to please my Father, but my flesh (our carnal nature) wants its own way. It seems to be the greatest battle within my mind. Have you ever felt like this? This will be one of your greatest struggles while on earth. As you allow the spirit of God to arise within you it will take over the flesh. Learning how to put your flesh to death will help diminish this struggle and will help you move down the dock of your destiny. This life will provide many opportunities for you to practice putting to death your flesh. A trip to the Yankari Game Reserve just happened to be one of those times for me!

MY FLESH FLIPS OUT ON THE YANKARI GAME RESERVE

We had just finished a series of meetings and were taking two days off to rest before the next set of meetings began. We were in Nigeria, Africa, and set out to visit the

Yankari Game Reserve. We were going to take in a safari! As we drove into the park, it was not at all what I had pictured. Then again, what is?

When we arrived at the reservation desk, we soon found out that our hotel room was accidentally given away to university students who were studying flowers. The management had to scramble to find us a place to stay. The park was full, and we had made reservations. We ended up staying in a round hut-type cabin located in their older, more desolate section of the park. From that moment I knew this was going to be a learning experience.

Interesting smells and bugs greeted us at the door of our temporary home away from home. I swallowed hard and went to the room assigned to me. Wise overseas travelers carry a sheet, pillowcase, and personal towel at all times. I was glad my mentor Dawn Lundgren clued me in on that little secret. Out came the linens and disinfectant. My flesh was crying, "I want to go home," but my spirit was saying, "Do not worry or be afraid, God knew you would be here at this time for this reason." So with that I went to sleep.

Good Morning Africa!

We all arose with the sun to go on our African safari through the game park. We would catch breakfast after our ride. The big open-back safari truck we were about to get on took close to five minutes to start. It sputtered and blew out black smoke several times as the driver tried to start it. This was a very good clue as to what was about to take place next. Unfortunately none of us were very bright detectives at that time in the morning. We all climbed up into the massive truck, held onto the bars for dear life, and proceeded into the jungle.

Monkeys, hippos, birds, and deer greeted us as we

drove through the beautiful jungle. It was exciting to travel through the jungle on this massive truck. Some of the wildlife found in this park included elephants, bush bucks, horned waterbucks, buffalo, lions, wart hogs, crocodiles, and baboons. This park has the largest elephant population in West Africa with a total of about 550. We were hoping to see a few of these on our safari.

About half way through the reserve, I could see a large mass of water ahead on the road and wondered if the truck could clear it. The driver obviously had faith in the truck making it through this mini lake because he began maneuvering it right through the water. However, half way through the truck became stuck in the sticky mud.

THERE GOES MY NICE BLUE FLIP-FLOPS

We sat and listened to the sounds of the jungle as we waited. It was a beautiful morning, and the birds and monkeys were busy chatting in the trees. The two guides tried everything they knew to do for this type of situation. Unfortunately calling a tow truck was not an option in the jungle. I just thought another truck would come and rescue us. Well, that did not happen. The next thing I heard was a conversation between the driver, our guide, and Dawn. I heard them speaking of us getting out of the truck. I was thinking, "No way!" I was not about to step into that mucky, murky lake of unknown. Besides I had on fancy blue flip-flops with colored beads.

Too bad for the flip-flops; when it was time to get out my name was called first. I was in a panic. We were in the middle of a jungle, stepping into who knows what, heading for who knows where. My imagination was going wild! I should have never watched Tarzan movies as a kid. What about those crocodiles they claim to have here? I clung on to the guide as he helped me out of the truck. I looked like a monkey as my arms were wrapped around his neck and my legs were around his waist trying to avoid any contact with the water. He shook me free and I landed in the water, blue flip-flops and all.

When we were all out of the truck and on dry ground, the guide told us we needed to walk back to the reserve. Everything in me was trying to hold back the fear I had of walking in a jungle with no gun, knife, or hubby to protect me. All of a sudden all of the animals I read about in the brochure came back to my memory. Up in the big truck I was brave and excited to see them. Now down at their level, I was scared and hoping they would not see us!

LIONS, TIGERS, AND BEARS… OH MY!

When we began walking, I stayed as close to the guide as I could. He had a big knife and I did not want to be at the tail end of our little human wagon train. No way! Especially when he told me animals were attracted to the color red. My friend Louise had on a red shirt and was walking in the back along with my other friend Barbara who could not walk very fast because of pain in her feet. Forget that business. I did not want to be some animal's lunch! It was always the slow and disabled lambs that were eaten in the storybooks I read as a kid. All I could hear was, "Lions, tigers, and bears…oh my!" from the Wizard of Oz.

My flesh was really showing its ugly side at this point. And I need to admit to you that I was not quick to repent of these stupid thoughts laced with fear. My flesh wanted to have a fit and pity party and I let it get the best of me. So, I walked in fear and pride for a mile or so not caring about anyone but me, myself and I—Oh my!

Then it happened. My fancy blue flip-flops with colored

beads began creating a sore in between my toes on each foot. The dirt collected from the trail we were walking on was rubbing against my skin where the rubber of my flip-flops touched my big toe. I thought, "Oh great! Not now! Oh please, God, help me!" I tried to ignore the pain, but in time I could not. I had to take off my flip-flops. This left me barefoot, in pain, and at the mercy of termites and red ants that like to bite. Walking barefoot on a stony path left me last in the line. I was right there in the back with Louise, her red shirt, and Barbara's sore feet.

At one point I stopped on the trail and cried out to God for grace and strength to make it. We were all getting weary and slowly became dehydrated because our water supply had run out. At this point I found my heart began to soften to the Lord, and saw I needed to repent of fear and pride. When I did I found a new grace to continue walking. It was like He provided His strength in my weakness and humility. I then wished I had done it way back in the beginning of this incredible learning experience. There is nothing like a barefoot walk in a hot jungle to kill the flesh.

We actually walked for a couple of hours before being rescued. The hot African sun was beating down on us as noontime approached. Our rescuers came in the form of about ten or so military police. When we saw the jeep coming our way I was jumping up and down on the path and waving my arms in joy. As the jeep speedily approached us and came to a sudden halt I had to jump out of its way and into the nearby bush not to be run over. You see, they thought we were poachers in the park stealing elephant tusks. They had no idea that we were just safari people stranded out in the jungle!

Once our guide told them who we were and what happened, they put away their machetes and guns. We instantly jumped into their jeep. They brought us back to the game reserve and dropped us off at the cafeteria. We all needed to drink water immediately. Once our bodies re-hydrated and cooled off, we could think more clearly. After lunch a few of us wanted to take a dip in the famous Wikki Waters of Nigeria located on the reserve grounds. This was a perfect opportunity to clean off the dirt and grime. It was also the perfect opportunity for my Father to teach me yet another valuable lesson.

WIKKI WATERS

The "Wikki Warm Springs" is famous for containing crystal-clear water from deep inside the earth. The water is as warm as a bathtub! This fresh water comes pouring out of a gigantic rock formation. From there it gushes as a waterfall and then flows out as a river. We swam at the very place the waters come out of the rock. It was one of the most unbelievable things I have seen with my own eyes and felt on my flesh. Many centuries ago hunters discovered these waters. Once the word was out, people from all over the world would go there to lie in the waters because of its healing properties.

God spoke to me while I floated in the Wikki Waters. I saw that I was not very quick to repent (to change my way of thinking) back in the jungle. I saw how I grumbled, felt sorry for myself, and was thinking more highly of myself than I should have. Our flesh will try and get in the way of quick repentance every time! Why did it take so long for me to see God? Because my flesh liked complaining—it felt good to have an attitude, it was covering up my fear of being eaten alive by some wild animal. I could have had a much better time in the jungle if I would have done things His way rather than walking in fear and pride.

He also spoke to me about Jesus being my Rock and out of Him flows fresh crystal-clear water. He showed me that the more I submerge myself in Him I would walk in complete healing in all areas of my life. Fear would have no place to hide in me if I completely submerge my life in Him. Since the hunters' discovery, The Wikki Waters dispelled fear and gave healing to the many sick pilgrims who visited there. Many diseases were cured when the people submerged themselves in the water containing high levels of pure minerals. Without repenting I would have missed this valuable lesson. I felt as though I was healed spiritually in those waters.

LESSONS FROM THE FATHER OFTEN ARE MISSED BECAUSE OF OUR FLESH

He spoke loud and clear to me that day in The Yankari Game Reserve. My flesh was weak, but He was strong. In this life there will be many times that you will not get your own way. How you handle yourself is important. If you choose the way of the flesh and find yourself "in the mucky jungle water," quick repentance is key to getting you back on the dock and hearing His voice clear again. The quicker the better! The Wikki Water is waiting. Take a dip and let the muck come off.

PERSONAL PRINCESS REFLECTIONS

1. Why does repentance help you stay on the dock and walk forward in your destiny?

2. Are you quick to repent? Do you repent even with your thought life?

3. What situation have you been in that was hard on your flesh and you wished it was not happening?

4. Did you learn anything from that experience?

5. Did you have to repent for having a bad attitude?

6. What portion of this chapter influenced you the most?

Chapter 10

PRINCESS KEY #3: THE HOLY SPIRIT

SO FAR YOU have learned that guarding your heart and repentance (changing your way of thinking) are two big keys to help you stay on the dock. They will get you back up and out of the water if you fall. There is one more key that pulls it all together and gives you the holding power to stay on the dock. It is the indwelling of the Holy Spirit. As stated in Acts 1:8 you will receive power when the Holy Spirit comes upon you. The power *Princess*!

THE HOLY SPIRIT

Without the Holy Spirit within you, your walk down the dock will be lifeless and dare I say—boring! The Holy Spirit gives you the holding power to stay on the dock. It is available to everyone in His Kingdom.

When I was about sixteen, I attended a weekly prayer meeting. At this particular meeting I was listening to a minister teach about the "Baptism of the Holy Spirit." He preached out of the Bible and showed us that John the Baptist was the first in the New Testament to speak about being baptized in the Holy Spirit. That is one reason he was called John the Baptist. Duh.

John would preach to his newly baptized followers and say, "I indeed baptize you with water; but One mightier than I is coming, Whose sandal strap I am not worthy to loose. He will baptize you with the Holy Spirit and with Fire." (See Luke 3:16.) John knew there was more than just water baptism. This was a heavy revelation at the time for many people. John knew that Jesus, the Messiah, was coming. So what was this Holy Spirit and fire stuff? The minister at the meeting explained it to us. I was on the edge of my seat!

THE HOLY SPIRIT IN JESUS WAS ACTIVATED

On the appointed day John baptized Jesus in the Jordan River. The Holy Spirit descended upon Jesus in bodily form like a dove and a voice came from heaven saying, "You are My Beloved Son; in You I am well pleased." (See Luke 3:22.) God the Father opened the heavens and gave Jesus, His Son, power from on high through the Holy Spirit. It is like the Holy Spirit was activated in Jesus that day. This was the beginning of Jesus' earthly ministry.

Jesus had the power of the Holy Spirit unleashed into Him so He could do the work He was called to do. His three and half years of ministry work, before He went to the cross, was empowered by the Holy Spirit. He taught His disciples about the kingdom of God, revealed Himself as the only way to the Father, and did signs and wonders among the crowds to deepen their faith in Him as the awaited Messiah. His main mission of dying on the cross for our sins, going to hell in our place, and rising again with the keys to hell in His hand was all empowered by the resurrection power of the Holy Spirit.

Then, as He was ascending into heaven after His resurrection from the dead, He told His disciples that He would send His Holy Spirit to be with them. He told them the Holy Spirit would now be their comforter, teacher, and guide. Jesus left them in the physical to live in them by the Spirit! I have great news for you. The same Spirit that raised Christ from the dead dwells in you! (See Acts 1:4–8.)

THE HOLY SPIRIT HELPS YOU SEE AND UNDERSTAND

When Jesus' ministry began, His disciples asked many, many questions. He was constantly explaining things to them about the kingdom of God. Most of the time they still had no clue what He was talking about! His words were a mystery and hidden from them, and they did not comprehend what He was telling them.

Jesus explained to them that after His ascension to heaven He would send His Holy Spirit to teach and guide them into all truths. So the disciples waited for this empowerment of the Holy Spirit that Jesus promised them as they gathered in a place called the "Upper Room". (See Acts 1:12–14.) They were all hiding. Up in the room they were seeking God together by prayer and worship when the Holy Spirit came upon them just like Jesus promised. Jesus sent the Holy Spirit on the day of Pentecost (A Jewish Feast Day) to the disciples. When the Holy Spirit empowered them, the eyes of their hearts were opened and they could finally see and understand all that Jesus was telling them before. Their understanding of the Kingdom of God became clear in that second.

The Bible says the Holy Spirit came in like a wind and you could see flames of Fire over their heads. John the Baptist spoke about that fire! (See Acts 2:1–4.) From that point on they did the works of Christ. They preached the Gospel of Christ, healed the sick, raised the dead, cleansed the lepers, and cast out demons everywhere they went. They were empowered with the Holy Spirit.

I Wanted This, Too!

As I listened to this preacher's message I began hungering for this empowerment of the Holy Spirit. Who wouldn't? Think about it. It says in Matthew 10:5-8 that Jesus charged his disciples to preach the gospel, heal the sick, raise the dead, cleanse the lepers, and cast out demons. Then to top it off, they baptized every new believer in the name of the Father, Son, and the Holy Spirit. (See Matthew 28:19.) What a way to walk the dock of your destiny!

I sat there that night and thought, "Sign me up for this Holy Spirit!" This was very exciting to me to hear this message. Finally, the power I was looking for to stay on the dock and be a strong anointed *Princess* was right before my eyes.

In the Book of Acts it says, "But you shall receive power when the Holy Spirit has come upon you." (See Acts 1:8.) Just as Jesus received power to fulfill His ministry on earth, we can receive the same resurrection power to fulfill our destiny while on earth. This same power breaks all strongholds in our lives. This is what I needed! His power from on High. I did not have this power in my own strength, the staying power to walk the dock!

Ask for the Indwelling Holy Spirit

The Holy Spirit comes and dwells in us when we ask Jesus into our lives. The Holy Spirit came with Jesus when I became a believer. As believers our bodies contain the Spirit of the Lord Jesus—His Holy Spirit. He is the Spring of Life. Jesus lives in us and through us by His Holy Spirit. However, just like a motor in a car needs to be turned on to have power to move, so it is with the Holy Spirit in us.

To activate means to start or turn on. You are baptized in the name of the Father, the Son, and the Holy Spirit.

As stated in Acts 2:1–4 the baptism with fire ignites the Holy Spirit in our lives. To ignite means to empower or super charge. The fire comes from asking for an impartation directly from Heaven. I figured that if Jesus and all the disciples were baptized in the water and then set on fire in the upper room, I wanted to do it, too! I wanted this—I needed this.

SO HOW DID I GET THE WATER AND FIRE BAPTISM?

At that weekly prayer meeting, leaders prayed for those of us that wanted the Holy Spirit to be ignited in our lives. This was done by the laying on of hands. This act is scriptural. (See Acts 8:14–17). I think I was first in line. The Holy Spirit that was living in me ignited. I was practically taken off my feet! I could totally relate to that car motor being turned on! I began to speak in an unknown language.

This is one of the manifest gifts of the Holy Spirit. Many people call it their heavenly prayer language. (See 1 Corinthians 12:7–11.) Some Christians believe that "speaking in tongues" is not for everyone and is one of the least important gifts of the Spirit. However, other Christians call themselves Spirit-filled believers and believe this gift stirs up the Holy Spirit inside of you. I use my prayer language in my personal time with the Lord. You may want to explore this concept further by reading what the Apostle Paul says about it in 1 Corinthians 14:18. He gives guidance as to the appropriateness of its use. Whether you speak in tongues or not, the Holy Spirit can be activated within you.

When the power of the Holy Spirit filled me, I was empowered from that moment on. Immediately I felt, saw, and walked in a different sensitive way than I had ever felt, saw, or walked. Receiving a heavenly prayer language was awesome! I have used this gift daily ever since. The Holy Spirit knows what and how to pray when we do not.

ONE DUNK WILL DO...

Then I had the opportunity to be baptized in water. The disciples were trained to baptize converts in water right away after their conversion to Christ. Jesus said to, "Go out, make disciples and baptize them in the name of the Father, the Son, and the Holy Spirit." This makes sense to me because it activates you right away to live as a *Princess* of the King. I wish I could have been symbolically baptized with water and fire right from the start in North Carolina. I did not experience fire baptism until a year later, and I was seventeen when I was baptized with water. Water baptism was so symbolic to me—leaving my old carnal flesh behind in the water and coming up a new creation in Christ. It helped me in my Christian walk.

Reverend Dave Roberson's book says it best: "Holy Spirit was with the Father and Son when you were being formed in your mother's womb. He knows your destiny and can pray you into your destiny better than you can. He knows all the days and plans for your life that were written in the book as the Father and Son formed you." Isn't that cool? I just love every part of the Holy Spirit.

STAYING ACTIVELY EMPOWERED BY THE HOLY SPIRIT

To stay actively empowered by the Holy Spirit, a few things are very helpful. We should praise, worship, pray, read the Word of God, and be still before Him. We need to spend time daily with the Father, Son, and Holy Spirit by reading and meditating. Ask Him daily to empower you anew! Just allow Him access to you every minute of every day—hearing Him in the life you live.

These things will fan that fire of the Holy Spirit. We must daily ask the Holy Spirit to breathe on that fire like a fan. Meditating on Scripture and a life of worship and prayer is the best fan you could own. We are held responsible to fan the flame. Once aflame you do not want to let it extinguish. My favorite time with the Lord is when I am taken away with Him into the heavenly realm and He begins to reveal His Kingdom to me. I love being with Him and soaking in His presence. This is where I find life. This life will fan the flame inside of you.

THE FATHER WANTS YOUR HEART

The Father is interested in your heart being aflame for Him. He wants to know you intimately and for you to know Him. All earthly things will pass away. The only thing that will remain is His love in us, and how we allowed it to work through us. Knowing Him and loving Him and others is His heart.

You cannot fake a pure heart and being the daughter in His Kingdom. Daughters with pure hearts hear God speak. Then He can direct and use you for His Kingdom purposes. The Holy Spirit helps us in both purity and in hearing His voice. Doing Kingdom work is awesome, but understanding and knowing you are a daughter of The Glorious King of Kings is priceless.

I am so glad I found the key of the Holy Spirit. This is the main key that will help you, too. You may have already found it, if not ask Him to show you the power of His Holy Spirit. Just say, "Father, I want it all as Your *Princess.* I need the full baptism of the Holy Spirit to come and fill me up."

He loves to hear us tell Him how much we need Him. He is our Father and loves to give us His good pleasures. Ask the Holy Spirit to be active in your life. Just ask and you will receive. It is the Father's good pleasure to give you His Kingdom!

I now had found that, even in my weakness, His Spirit would carry me. His activated and ignited Spirit in me was the strength and grace to fight off fleshly desires and temptations of sin that all too often made me slip. All of us have fleshly desires and temptations we must deal with, but with the power of the Holy Spirit we have the victory.

The Car Crash

One frozen winter morning I was in my car and on my way home from a dentist appointment. My mouth was numb from Novocain. The roads were slippery from an ice storm. Somehow I lost control of my van and began spinning in circles. My spinning came to a halt when another truck slammed into my side. All the while I was calling out to Jesus.

I climbed out of my van, looked at the damage, and then walked over to the other vehicle. The lady in the truck was shaking uncontrollably. I thought that maybe she was injured. When she assured me she was not injured, I invited her over to my van to wait for the police. The wait ended up being at least an hour long because of all the accidents across the city that morning.

We sat in my warm van and chatted about our families while we waited. She looked at me and said, "Why are you so peaceful?" With that kind of question I knew she could see the fruit of the Holy Spirit in me and was curious. I began to tell her how Jesus was my peace. She began to weep. I told her she could have this peace in her life, too.

Just then the police pulled up. I thought, "Wouldn't you know it; she asks me this awesome question just as the police car drives up." We got out of my van and sat in the back seat of the police car. While sitting in the back seat answering insurance questions, I was also inquiring of the Lord about our little situation at hand. I said, "Lord, You know why she asked me that question. How am I supposed to tell her about you now that she is out of my van?" He said, "Tell her it was no accident that she ran into you today." Wow, what a line! Only God could have come up with that one. But when should I tell her? Would I get another opportunity?

The wind was blowing like crazy, with freezing rain outside when we got out of the police car. We both headed for our vehicles. I barely heard her saying something to me. So I said, "What? I cannot hear you." So she came over to my van and I told her to jump in. She needed my telephone number for insurance stuff. So I gave it to her and then knew it was the time to tell her what God told me to say. So I did. I told her that the Father loved her and He wanted her to know that it was no accident that she ran into me today. She started to cry again. I then prayed with her to have Jesus as her Peace in life. The Holy Spirit living in me was apparent to her in the form of peace during a crisis. Because I was filled, I could give it out.

Someone who carries the Holy Spirit stands out to non-believers during stressful times. It then becomes something they desire. I saw this truth again when our city was hit with two hurricanes. The world cannot offer this kind of peace. This is why you want to remain filled. It is not only for your benefit, but also for others to see God. You are the vessel God wants to use to touch the world. The Holy Spirit working through you will help others find their dock of destiny in God's kingdom.

Personal Princess Reflections

1. What are the three keys from Chapters 8, 9, and 10 to help you stay on the dock walking in your destiny?

   1). G____________ your heart.

   2). Quick R____________.

   3). Being filled with the H____________ S___________.

2. Have you been baptized in water?

3. How about the fire? Write out the experience.

4. How does the Holy Spirit empower you to do the work of the gospel?

5. How do you continue to fan the flame to keep the fire?

6. Do you have a special time with the Father, Son, and the Holy Spirit everyday? If not what is hindering you?

7. What did you personally receive out of this chapter?

Chapter 11

It Is Time for You to Walk the Dock

Remember the ugly witch in the Disney movie *Snow White*? She would look into her mirror and ask it, "Who is the fairest of them all?" She apparently was clueless as to who she was and where she was going. We have so many benefits in being a daughter of the King. We know who we are and where we are going. We do not go to a mirror for our identity, nor should we go to anyone other than the Lord.

In 2 Corinthians 3:18, (nkjv) the Bible says, "But we all, with unveiled face, beholding as in a mirror the glory of the Lord, are being transformed into the same image from glory to glory just as by the spirit of the Lord." The greatest characteristic you can show, as a *Princess* in the Kingdom is this completely unveiled openness before the King. By doing this, your life becomes a mirror for others to see Christ.

Others will be able to tell if you have been beholding the Lord. You will mirror the Lord's own character. Your likeness will be like Christ. You will not be offended easily and will forgive quickly. You will allow the Lord into the dark places of your heart and stay pure before Him. Your mirror is not cloudy or dirty. You will become a transparent *Princess* with no pride or boasting in yourself. You will shine like the brightness of the noonday.

Humility will be your cloak of choice. Your life in Him becomes as natural as breathing. As you stay in His presence you will be a mirror for others to behold the glory of the Lord. Without abiding in His presence and obeying all His ways you will soon forget who you are and where you are going. That is when you begin to look into other mirrors to find yourself. Let Him be your only mirror. This is one of the greatest truths I have learned in my walk.

CAR CRASH—AGAIN

It was a cool fall morning when I dropped my two older kids off at computer school. It was also my older daughter Sophia's birthday. Her birthday landed on *Rosh Hashanah,* which is a corporate day of repentance in the Jewish religion.

On my way home I was approaching a yield sign and tried to slow down. When I put on my brakes nothing happened. My brakes went to the floor, but my van just kept rolling at about ten miles an hour. I began crying out to Jesus. The car in front of me had stopped and I was headed right for it.

My van hit the back bumper of the car. With that I knew I had to get out and survey the damage. This would be no problem in a perfect world. But, you see, that particular morning I went buzzing out of my house wearing my leopard print flannel pajamas, fuzzy leopard print slippers, and my husband's blue sweatshirt. I had on no make-up and had "bed hair". Now, with that, I shuddered thinking about stepping out of my car and meeting this girl. Talk about wearing the cloak of humility.

Do you remember that I pray in tongues when I do not know what to pray? Phoebe, who was seven at the time, became my instant intercessor for the situation and we both broke into praying in our heavenly language. Yes, even at the dear age of seven, Phoebe used her heavenly language like a seasoned prayer warrior.

I mustered up the courage to get out of my car to assess damage and speak to the girl. She was a beautiful young girl on her way to work. Immediately I noticed she had a fat lip and cut on her face. I asked her if she was okay. She said she was fine and the damage on her face was from the previous night. I thought to myself, "What happened to her?"

There was no damage to her car or my van so we did not need to call the police. I told her about my brakes not working. She offered to drive in front of me to a gas station. I was so grateful for her offer. Phoebe and I drove slowly behind her car. My brakes now seemed to be working just fine. At the station I thanked her for helping me. I told her she was so beautiful I was wondering what nationality she was. She told me she was half-Jewish and half-African American. As she spoke, I knew this was another divine appointment.

HER LIFE STORY WAS REVEALED

At that time I co-hosted a television show called "Focus on Israel," so I was somewhat knowledgeable about Judaism. I told her that her nationality was revealed to me for a reason. I then asked her if she practiced her Judaism. With that comment she began telling me about her life right there in the gas station parking lot.

Her mother no longer practiced the Jewish customs; her father was a Christian. Her parents were now divorced. She professed to be a Christian in a backslidden state. The damage on her face was from the father of her baby. They were not married. He became angry and hit her. She told me she had not slept all night because of the abuse. She was clearly frazzled and tired. She began to choke up. I asked her, "Do you realize what day it is?" She shook her head no. I told her, "Today is Rosh Hashanah, the Jewish day of repentance for sin." She again had big tears. I explained how God still loved her and never left her even though she felt far away from Him. The Shepherd cares for the one lost sheep that strays from the fold. Today He was calling her back to Himself.

I prayed over her and knew that it was another divine appointment and not an accident! I told her that God had more for her than to be beat up by some guy. She said, "I used to go to a really on-fire church. But ever since I met him my life has been hell." I was there to encourage her to run back into the Father's arms. It was there that she would find safety and comfort. She and I both knew it was God that orchestrated our meeting. We hugged, said good-bye, and drove away. From that point on my brakes worked just fine.

Humility was the cloak I wore that day; but God used it to bring another little lamb home to His side. Stay in His presence, obey His Word, and you will be a mirror for others to behold the glory of the Lord. It is time for you to watch for those divine appointments that happen as you walk your dock. Do not let the leopard print pajamas and "bed hair" stop you from being the vessel the Father wants to use at any given moment.

Stay open before the Lord with your life and you will stay on the dock as His *Princess.* Continue being filled by His Spirit so His liquid fire of love will pour out to a lost and dying world. Make Him a proud daddy of a precious *Princess.* Become the *Princess* that knows who she is and where she is going by only looking to Him.

LET HIM OUT

Jesus wants to come forth in you and touch the world around you. Let Him out. He is the vine and you are the branches. It is like having the Tree of Life living and growing within you. Let that Tree of Life grow and take over your earthen vessel. Its branches (you) will be a refuge for others to find rest and shade from this life. And Life overrides death. Light overtakes darkness. This Tree of Life will overshadow death in every area of your life and in others, if you let it grow. When you begin to understand that He is all about Life you will smell death even when it is ten feet away. The way to this truth is in beholding Him, looking at Him, and seeing Him in His beauty. The more time I spend resting in His presence, the more at home I feel in that heavenly realm of glory. It is the realm in which we will all live in forever and ever. So why not begin to experience it now, the early church did. I think it is all up to us. That is cool.

PERSONAL PRINCESS REFLECTIONS

1. What do you see when you look in the mirror?

2. What will help you be more sensitive to the Holy Spirit when He is showing you a divine appointment?

3. Have you ever had a divine appointment?

4. Do you want one?

5. Have you ever taken the time to just rest in Him and see Him for who He was?

6. If so, did He reveal Himself to you in a greater manner?

7. What impacted you the most in this chapter?

Chapter 12

GOING INTO YOUR WORLD

FELLOW *PRINCESS*, I may never have the pleasure of meeting you here while on this earth or chat with you online, but that is okay because we will have eternity to talk about everything! I thought you would be interested in finishing that instant messaging chat I had with that Junior High cool group *Princess*. She was just going to tell me what happened to change her life when she turned fourteen:

RRR1963: i finally understood who i was and where i was going—amazingly so, the turmoil during jr. high made my heart soft towards receiving help. i was unhappy, insecure, and lonely. i knew i needed help—i found this help in God—through this relationship with God the Father, and His Son Jesus, i have found my true identity, calling, and destiny on this earth—it was just the help i needed.

Me: sounds like U found a new social group! LOL!

RRR1963: 4 sure…i did! Yeah—it is called the kingdom of God—in that kingdom i am a daughter of the Most High King—that makes me a *Princess*—cause daughters of Kings are *Princesses*—LOL!

Me: cool—i bet U wish U belonged way B4 U were 14...

RRR1963: yeah—that's Y i've made it my job now 2 inform younger women about the kingdom of God so they can make it through those years successfully with the grace of a *Princess*—and go on 2 their destiny and calling—this simple revelation of my royalty in God's Kingdom has completely changed the way i think about myself. the security of knowing i am His royal child has changed the way i think and act towards others. this kingdom revelation i now understand has made, and still is making, a lasting impact in my life as a wife, mother, minister, daughter, friend, neighbor, and citizen. it is time 4 us as women 2 come forward and become everything our Father has made us 2 B. i want 2 reveal 2 these young woman the royal inheritance they have received in this supernatural Kingdom of God.

Me: very cool—but I think any age woman can benefit from this message!sounds like Ur on a mission—so glad we could chat—what an awesome opportunity U have 2 teach younger women...but do not forget us older ones...LOL. thanks 4 taking the time 2 answer my lingering questions! LOL!

RRR1963: yep!

Me: g2g—

RRR1963:ttyl—ciao!

It easy for me to chat with "RRR1963". In case you did not realize it, the "RRR1963" is actually me, interviewing myself with instant messaging. LOL! RRR1963 are my initials and the year I was born.

I have shown you how to share your walk down the dock (or whatever your runway may be) by sharing my walk with you. Now it is your turn to do the same. Go out and tell others the good news of this kingdom. God is calling you to encourage other *Princesses* in the kingdom of God.

ONE LAST STORY—GO TELL OTHERS

While ministering in Riga, Latvia, a group of us went into the old city to get a feel for the people and the area. We found an open market and began to pray and talk as we walked. We came upon an elderly lady on the corner selling plastic shopping bags. She was obviously poor, wore tattered clothes, and her wrinkled face was tanned from the sun. She asked us if we would buy a bag from her.

We had an interpreter with us because we did not speak Russian, and I spoke to this woman through our interpreter. I told her I wanted to buy a couple of bags. She smiled and said, "Thank you." I told the interpreter to tell her that she was special to God and that He loved her. Just minutes earlier I had purchased some flowers, so I gave her some of them. With that she looked at me, and I watched big tears begin to roll down her weathered cheeks. I continued to speak words of life to her because her heart was obviously soft. We not only had the opportunity to pray with her and tell her about Jesus, but we asked the Holy Spirit to touch her mightily. She could barely talk when we left. All of us were deeply touched by this woman's sincere response to the Father, Son, and Holy Spirit.

We left the market area and walked and prayed some more. Eventually we found ourselves in the oldest part of the city on a street made of bricks. From a distance I could hear and see two girls sitting on the sidewalk playing guitars. As we came closer, I assumed they were blind. I asked the interpreter if the blind girls were playing for money. She said, "What blind girls?" I pointed and said, "Those blind girls." Their eyes almost glowed they were so white. She looked at me like I was silly and told me that they were not blind at all. Then I knew it had to be God speaking to me.

LOOK AGAIN

I sensed the Holy Spirit saying to me, "Look again. They are blind to the Spirit of God and need you to give them sight." I shared this revelation with the group as we approached the two girls. We walked up to them and began a conversation. Just as we began to speak to them about God, four young men came out of nowhere and were headed straight towards us. They rather abruptly asked the one girl if they could play her guitar. She seemed a bit confused. She obviously did not know these boys. It was odd and tense. Out of fear she reluctantly handed over her guitar. I sensed that they were a diversion from the enemy to stop God's divine plan of salvation for two new *Princesses* to His Kingdom.

As the boy strummed the guitar, I asked the Lord for a song. I shut my eyes and began to sing (as loud as I could) a prophetic song of hope and love over the city of Riga. With no interpreter they were clueless as to what I was singing. Then I sang out, "Jesus loves you this I know." The boy stopped playing, turned whiter than a sheet and practically threw the guitar back to the girl. All four of them ran down the street. It happened so quickly that we were startled! Once the intruders were gone, we led both girls to Jesus and told them about the Kingdom of God. They cried when we prayed. I gave the remainder of my flowers to the two girls. The mission was complete.

That day was divinely appointed by my Father. God the Father is the Almighty Creator and He has many exciting missions for you also. It never has to be a dull and boring life on earth.

TIME FOR YOU TO WALK THE DOCK

Rest in Him and watch as He reveals these glorious plans to you. Never stop seeking Him with your whole heart, spirit, body, mind, and soul. Always keep before you the truth that you are deeply loved by the Father, you are special to Him and part of His royal family. Remember, Jesus, His Son, is waiting patiently for the day that you come to Him in fullness as His bride to rule and reign with Him for eternity. The Prince awaits your arrival.

Walk in obedience to God's Word, with your head held high in confidence, empowered by the Holy Spirit knowing you are a His daughter and promised to Jesus. Jesus made the way, so go for it! The dock of destiny is just waiting for you to continue your walk. So walk on *Princess*...

PERSONAL PRINCESS REFLECTIONS

1. When you think of your future, what do you see?

2. Have you seen glimpses of your destiny? Write down what you feel He has revealed to you about your destiny here on earth.

3. Be honest about your relationship with Jesus, the Son of God—where are you in your relationship?

4. Do you want more of Him and to know Him better? Ask Him to do that for you.

5. Are there areas that you would like to see Him come into and share with you? List them.

6. Explain how this book has impacted your thinking about His Kingdom here on earth.

7. If you could share this book with one other person, who would it be? Send it to them.

NOTES

CHAPTER 2

THE FIRST ROYAL FAMILY

1. Bruce Lansky, *The Very Best Baby Name Book* (Minnetonka, MN: Meadow Brook Press, 1996).

CHAPTER 3

CINDERELLA: THE FICTIONAL *PRINCESS*

1. Author's paraphrase of "Cinderella" by Walt Disney, 1954.

CHAPTER 4

WHAT DOES A *PRINCESS* LOOK LIKE?

1. *NIV Bible Dictionary* (Grand Rapids, MI: Zondervan,1987).

CHAPTER 7

REST IN YOUR ROYALTY

1. Joyce Meyers, *Me and My Big Mouth* (Tulsa, OK: Harrison House, 1996).

CHAPTER 10

PRINCESS KEY #3: THE HOLY SPIRIT

1. Rev. Dave Roberson, *The Walk of the Spirit—the Walk of Power*, Dave Roberson Ministries, 1999.

About the Author

Robin R. Rinke, founder of Freebird Ministries, has traveled internationally, preaching the Word and leading revelatory worship. She is a transparent, passionate, and humorous minister. Everything in her life flows out of intimacy with the Lord.

She is a devoted wife and mother, has recorded several original CDs, and has hosted two Christian television broadcasts.

Robin holds *Princess* Seminars and conferences to help young women take hold of their inheritance and walk in their destiny as daughters of God. Through the Word and worship they awaken in His endless love and learn to walk in newfound freedom.

Robin and her husband, Chuck, live and minister in South Florida with their three children, Samuel, Sophia, and Phoebe.

Freebird Ministries Information

Web Site:
www.freebirdministries.org
Email:
princessrobin@freebirdministries.org

To Order *The Making of a Princess* Book or Music CDs:

Call Toll Free: (866) 572-7665 or (719) 488-4366
Office Hours: 9:00 a.m. - 5:00 p.m.
Mon.-Fri. Mountain Time Zone

Write: Lakeland Leadership League
1840 Woodmoor Dr.
Suite 100
Monument, CO 80132

Visit Web Site: www.lakelandleadership.com/store.html